Love in the Mortar Joints

Love in the Mortar Joints

The Story of Habitat for Humanity

By
MILLARD FULLER
and
Diane Scott

Association Press
NEW WIN PUBLISHING, INC.

Designed by Karen A. Yops

Cover photo: Bob Hooley-Gingrich, a Mennonite from Indiana; Arthur Pless, a member of the A.M.E. Church from Georgia; and Martha Cruz, an American Baptist from New York, work on the housing project in Americus, Georgia. Photo by Wayne Perkins

Printing Code

23 24 25 26 27 28 29 30

Library of Congress Catalog Card Number: 81-86084

ISBN 0-8329-1444-4

Printed in United States of America.

This book is dedicated, with deepest gratitude,
to the host of Habitat partners everywhere,
whose faithful prayers and support
continue to make this venture grow.
For each one of you, we thank and praise the Lord.

Contents

Foreword

By all measures, this is an extraordinary story—the more so, because it is true. I know it is true because I have had the privilege of having a ringside seat for many of the events described in this book.

In writing the foreword to this book by my friend Millard Fuller, I have a problem. How does one describe this book? It is the story of one man's journey of faith. It is also the story of an era in our nation's history. At the same time, it is a prophetic book, suggesting something of the shape of the future for our nation and for the church of Jesus Christ. Above all, it is the story of God's continuing action in the affairs of men and women.

Beyond these broader dimensions, the book deals specifically and tellingly with the financial, sociological, psychological, and political implications of the Gospel. Millard's story could even be called a case study in holistic medicine, not unlike Norman Cousins's best-selling book *The Anatomy of an Illness.* It suggests that the causes for many of our illnesses are spiritual and that the cure must also be spiritual.

Perhaps the best way to incoporate all that I've said so far is to liken *Love in the Mortar Joints* to a continuation of the New Testament Book of Acts. It reads like fifteen subsequent chapters dealing with the acts of the Holy Spirit in the affairs of people today. For many of us, the Book of Acts is a romantic, fanciful, and wistful story. We wish things were still like that. Well, Millard Fuller's book gives us hope. Things have not changed. God is still dealing with people and with groups as He did in that marvelous chronicle of the early church.

I remember being invited many years ago to preach the centennial sermon at a church in Bermuda. On that Sunday the governor of Bermuda was present. I still remember my text: the account in the Gospel of Mark of Jesus' calling four particular fishermen by name, saying simply, "Follow me!" I suggested through the use of several stories that Jesus still calls men and women today, with the same results.

As the governor left the church and shook my hand, he said these unforgettable words: "I really enjoyed your sermon. I only wish it were true."

It *is* true. Millard Fuller heard the call of Jesus to follow Him, and he did. *Love in the Mortar Joints* is the record of some of the things that have happened to him—and through him to others all over the world—because he responded affirmatively to that call.

I believe one of the key problems for Christians in today's church is to decide whether to deify Jesus or to obey Him. Millard's story, like that of Zacchaeus in the New Testament, is the story of repentance and obedience. Like Zacchaeus, Millard finds that God offers him love and forgiveness. His response is to give away most of what he possesses—in Millard's case, a million dollars.

I would like to add a personal note here. I read the manuscript for this book at a time when I was also faced with making a change. I felt that Jesus was calling me to a new place in life where I would have less rather than more—less money, less leisure, less privacy, less comfort, less security. Reading this book helped me greatly. God spoke to me through it about His call to all of us at all times.

I have a dream for the church of Jesus Christ. I believe that every Christian has a destiny. Like Mother Teresa in Calcutta, each one of us has a place with his or her name on it where God's people are hurting. If we hear the call of Christ and respond, He will send us, with joy and abandon, to lift burdens and to liberate people. This book will show many believers how to find their particular Calcutta. People today are looking for fulfillment; this book holds the key to that fulfillment. When she received her Nobel Prize, Mother Teresa reminded us: "The poor don't need us. We need the poor."

Herein lies the secret of spiritual fulfillment. *Love in the Mortar Joints* will bring life and hope and fulfillment to many, through many others who hear and understand and obey.

Bruce Larson
Pastor, University Presbyterian Church
Seattle, Washington
Author, past president of
Faith at Work

Acknowledgments

The story you are about to read is told by me; the research and writing have been done in collaboration with Diane Scott of Salem, New Jersey. I wrote the story over a period of eighteen months in such diverse places as my office and home in Americus, Georgia; a hotel room in Nairobi, Kenya; on *many* airplanes flying to and from speaking engagements all over the United States and Canada and especially on two long trips—to Puerto Rico, Colombia, and Guatemala in 1978 and to Kenya, Zambia, and Zaire in 1979; and in a small beachfront cottage south of Tallahassee, Florida. But that manuscript is not what you will read. Diane Scott, who gave so much of herself in the rewriting and editing of my first book, *Bokotola* (Association Press/Follett, 1977), worked for many months to put this new story together in its final form. I do not have adequate words with which to acknowledge properly her tremendous contribution in making this book a reality.

Like everything that Habitat for Humanity does, however, *Love in the Mortar Joints* is the result of a partnership of *many* volunteers. Without the help of all these people, this story and this book would not have been possible.

Even though any list would be inadequate, Diane and I would like especially to thank the following persons for their unique contributions:

Jean Johnson and Caryl Slifer, who typed feverishly on the manuscript in New Jersey.

My wife Linda, and Joyce Hollinger Haller, who typed the final manuscript in Georgia.

Susan Ausley, in Florida, whose beachfront cottage offered a blessedly quiet refuge where I could relax and work on the book.

Jim and Janette Prickett, whose talents and dedication kept the busy Habitat office functioning so smoothly that Linda and I could take off occasionally to spend the many hours necessary to write the original draft.

Diane's husband, Vic Scott, who did the same for her in the office of their nursery farm in New Jersey, all the while providing steadfast encouragement and perceptive literary criticism.

Sam Emerick, whose faithful and capable leadership as president of Habitat for Humanity's board of directors has been a guiding force behind the whole evolving ministry, helping, in a powerful way, to bring this story to life.

Thomas McFarland, my law partner, who carried the full load of the law office while I was away working on the manuscript or involved in other activities of Habitat for Humanity, especially the frequent speaking trips.

Jean Lesher of Association Press/Follett Publishing Company in Chicago, whose efforts in the production of this book went far beyond what her job would have required.

All biblical quotations used throughout this book are taken from the *Good News Bible* published by the American Bible Society, New York.

All revenues, including royalties, from the sale of this book will go directly into the support of this blossoming ministry. If this story excites your imagination, I hope you will "pass it on" by sharing this book with all who might want to become involved.

Millard Fuller
Americus, Georgia
May 1980

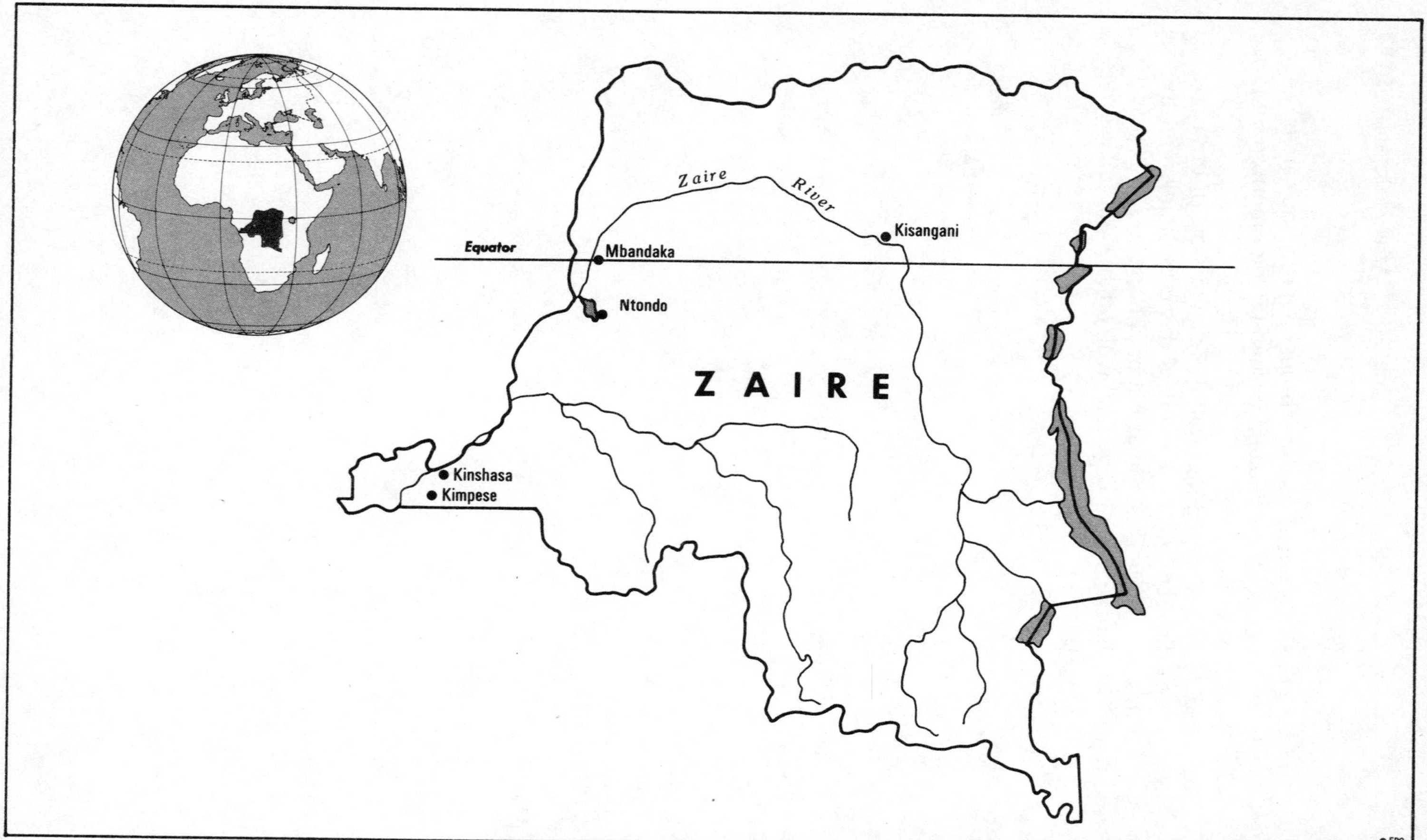

ZAIRE
Zaire River
Kisangani
Equator
Mbandaka
Ntondo
Kinshasa
Kimpese

1
Jubilation in a Jungle Village

Ninety miles to go. And the trip would take at least four hours.

Sitting on our bags in the back of a pickup truck, we bounced over the dusty, rutted dirt roads in the company of seven other passengers, their luggage, and their livestock. Four of the people also carried babies. Because we were right on the African equator and it was just after lunchtime, the temperature was perhaps 95° F. and the humidity was about the same percent. It may not sound exactly like the journey of your dreams.

But for me it was just that—the exciting, long-anticipated trip of a lifetime, and the fulfillment of a dream.

The date was July 7, 1979. Three years earlier my wife Linda and I, with our four children, had left this struggling young country of Zaire (formerly the Belgian Congo) to return home to the United States. There we hoped to be able to raise more funds and to expand in other areas the concept of self-help community building for poverty families, which we had labored to establish in Zaire.

From 1973 to 1976 we had worked in the sprawling city of

Mbandaka, inaugurating a program to construct decent, sturdy cement-block homes for poor families formerly consigned to miserable mud shacks. These homes would instantly be rejected by most North Americans and Europeans as too primitive. Simple one-story structures with cement slab floors and tin roofs, most had three small bedrooms and a separate kitchen area to keep the wood fires from smoking up the other rooms. No electricity. No plumbing. But no more vermin-infested thatch roofs either. No puddles on dirt floors for mosquito-breeding havens; no mud walls progressively disintegrating with each succeeding storm. To many desperately poor citizens of Mbandaka, the opportunity to build and own a solid house had brought real hope for the first time in their lives.*

We had left Mbandaka on July 5, 1976. Now, three years later almost to the day, Linda and I had returned to survey the growth of this development, where 100 homes were now complete and occupied by families of ten to fifteen people each. We had found a thriving community of landscaped houses sparkling with fresh paint, immaculate and cared for with obvious pride. We inspected many more homes still under construction. That visit had been a tremendous thrill.

The best part of our trip, however, was yet to come. Our destination on that hot afternoon was a long-awaited celebration.

When we left Zaire in 1976, the little jungle village of Ntondo, ninety miles down the Zaire River from Mbandaka, was just beginning its own building project. Even poorer than the residents of Mbandaka, the people in Ntondo had nevertheless eagerly latched on to an exciting possibility: that by working faithfully with God and each other, they might actually be able to rebuild completely their village of 3,000 people, one house at a time. They were encouraged by an outstanding local leader, Mompongo Mo Imana—known to everyone as Sam—who had been able to come to the United States and receive a university education (he speaks six languages) and who had then returned to the interior to help his own people.

---

* The complete story of our African experience is told in *Bokotola,* Chicago, Association Press, 1977.

The citizens of Ntondo, in a mass meeting at the local church in June of 1976, had voted unanimously to launch out in faith. They would embark on a project to build a solid house for every single family who needed one—and that meant *every* family in the village except three! If there were widows or elderly people who were unable to contribute to the financing of their homes, then the rest, out of their already pitifully meager resources, would find ways to assist.

When we left Zaire a month later, the people of Ntondo were already stockpiling impressive quantities of sand and gravel in three locations. The huge piles looked even more impressive when we realized that every grain and pebble was hauled as much as half a mile up from Lake Tumba, at the edge of town, in a homemade bark basket balanced on someone's head! The townspeople had also raised $2,000 to begin buying cement. And Ken Sauder, a Mennonite volunteer from Mt. Joy, Pennsylvania, who had been working with us in Mbandaka, had moved to Ntondo to help launch the new venture.

Could anyone start with $2,000 and some piles of sand and build enough houses for 3,000 people? The villagers in Ntondo believed that this miracle could happen—and so did I.

After Linda and I had returned to the United States in 1976, I often spoke before church groups about what was happening in Ntondo. Already, under the leadership of Sam Mompongo, the people had erected their own high school. It is a handsome building accommodating 700 students, and dormitories have been constructed to house young people who must travel long distances. That project took eight years. Since then Sam had also coordinated the building of six junior high schools in surrounding villages, all of which now send students to Ntondo for secondary education.

As I talked to churches and concerned individuals in America, many were moved to help. Before long, funds had been raised to buy Ntondo a dump truck. When it finally arrived, after months of frustrating red tape, it was received with great celebration—and the buckets-on-the-head process was speeded up considerably.*

---

* A letter from Sam Mompongo, dated March 6, 1978, described the excitement occasioned by the truck's arrival: "It was about 4 P.M. on Sunday, February 26, when the orange 7.6-ton dump truck emerged in Ntondo. The

Often an American or Canadian church, upon learning that an African family could move out of a crumbling shack into a solid home for only $2,000, would decide, "Let's build a house!" and the funds for one more eagerly awaited home were on the way. Volunteers from many denominational backgrounds had traveled to Ntondo to help, staying for periods of from six weeks to two years. And Sam Mompongo had come to America in 1976 and again in the fall of 1978, crisscrossing the country to speak to scores of church and civic groups, generating still more support for the rebuilding of his town.

I knew that big things had been happening in the village of Ntondo. But knowing wasn't the same as being there. Now, a service of dedication had been planned for Sunday, July 8, 1979, and we were on our way to participate.

Linda and I had traveled from our home in Americus, Georgia. With us was Donna Stevens, of Angola, Indiana, a widowed mother of six and grandmother of eight. Donna had volunteered to come at her own expense to take slides for publicity and fund raising. (Well, Linda and Donna weren't exactly *with* the rest of us, since they had been granted the choice seats in the truck's cab!)

The fourth member of our party was Geoff Van Loucks, an attorney from Los Gatos, California. A tremendous supporter of the building project through his United Church of Christ congregation in San José, Geoff had decided he would travel halfway around the world with us, also at his own expense, to see firsthand what was evolving in this small African village.

Throughout those four jarring hours I clung to the back of the jammed pickup truck as we plunged from one pothole to another. Every joint in my body, I felt sure, must be audibly creaking. At the same time, I found I also had to deal with the extraordinary pounding of my heart. After traveling

---

whole community had been waiting for the vehicle since noon. As the truck came in sight the church bell rang and men, women, and children stormed the streets, running toward the junction of Melika Lane (the town's main street, a corruption of the word "America") and the road from Mbandaka. As the vehicle stopped at the market place, a group of women appeared in parade, singing joyfully 'we are off to do the work of the Lord' and praising God for the fine and kind people of America. It was one of our most exciting moments. . . ."

nearly 7,000 miles for this occasion, I felt almost like a child on Christmas Eve—certain, after a very long wait, that there was something really wonderful in store, and impatient to know everything about it right away!

About five miles south of Mbandaka we rode through the little village of Bolenge. I noticed again the graveyard where Joseph Clarke, a pioneering American Baptist missionary, is buried. The elementary school in Ntondo is named for him. I remembered that when Clarke started home to retire in 1930, after fifty years in Zaire, he got as far as Bolenge and died. Those who knew him well said that he never wanted to leave his African friends anyway. I could understand that.

Next came Secli-Wenji. We turned left. Then Kalamba. A right turn here, and the truck leaned precariously under its load. Small villages continued to appear every few miles along the way, most of them only one house deep. With rare exceptions the houses were made of the standard mud bricks, or mud and sticks, with a flimsy palm thatch roof. Behind the houses the immense, thick rain forest closed in, and where there were no villagers living to keep the shoulders cleared, we couldn't see ten feet back from the road.

We turned left again, and the road got rougher. We were traveling through a big rubber plantation, past row upon endless row of rubber trees on both sides of the road. I remembered stories of the early part of this century, when Zaire was the Belgian Congo. At that time the forests had been full of wild rubber vines. The raw rubber was just like money hanging from trees, and the colonizers had forced the natives to gather it. Those who didn't meet their quotas sometimes had hands chopped off, or were simply lined up and shot. My friends in Ntondo had often told me of those bleak days. Now they were over; the rubber vines were gone, and the sticky stuff presently came from large spreads of cultivated trees.

It was almost dark when we finally rounded the last curve at the edge of Ntondo. By this time, the eager thoughts that filled my head were just about drowned out by the painful complaints that kept coming from the rest of me!

Suddenly, aches and fatigue vanished. As we faced the entrance to the town, we met two freshly painted signs, one in English and the other in French, that said, WELCOME TO THE NEW NTONDO! I peered into the twilight as far as I could see beyond these signs, and I could already count at least twenty new houses in a variety of bright colors.

A barrier of palm branches had been placed across the road, and several men were stationed beside it. As soon as the truck came to a halt, one of the men began blowing a signal on an antelope horn. Instantly, people were pouring out of the nearby houses, and more came running down the roads from the center of the village.

Two chairs appeared from somewhere, and Linda and I were instructed to sit down right on the spot. For the next several minutes, in the midst of an excited, steadily enlarging crowd, we received vigorous handshakes, bear hugs, and official welcomes, in that order. First, from wonderful Pastor Ngando, who has ministered to the people of Ntondo for *fifty-nine* years, and then from Sam Mompongo. At last they indicated that we should all proceed together into the center of the village.

I believe that that walk, covering perhaps half a mile, was the most incredible hour any of us had ever experienced. As Geoff said afterward, "I felt like a victorious general returning in triumph to his native city!"

At first, there were hundreds of men and boys crowding around us, singing, shouting, dancing, clapping, praising the Lord. Then the number of people abruptly doubled as a great wave of women, singing in organized groups, came toward us. We moved very slowly, because everyone wanted to shake hands, to shout a greeting, to point out something we simply must see. At one of the first spanking-new houses we passed, the proud owner clutched me and jumped up and down again and again. He couldn't stop. He was absolutely beside himself with enthusiasm—*he had a decent home!*

The cacophony of sound around us was deafening, and I was just as glad. At several points along the way, I simply could not have spoken to anyone. The joy around us was too overwhelming. My throat choked up, and my eyes flooded with tears.

Just three years before, this village had been a collection of dismal shacks. Now, as we walked slowly on, we viewed one new house after another along both sides of the road. Some were finished and gaily painted, with the old houses in front of them or beside them in various stages of falling down or being torn down; many other homes were still under construction. The startling transformation taking place in Ntondo, accompanied by the incredible jubilation of the villagers, was as moving a sight as anything I had ever witnessed.

By the time we got into the village center, there were perhaps 2,000 people with us. Here some of the town's leaders stood waiting, accompanied by two beaming little girls who presented to Linda and me large bouquets of pink and white wild flowers gracefully arranged with greens from the forest. Surely, this was a welcome we'd never forget.

Mounted on two big posts behind this official welcoming committee was a large and colorful sign showing the plan for the new Ntondo. It was a greatly magnified version of the original survey made by volunteer Ryan Karis in 1977. The diagram showed that houses had been started on 110 of the 300 neatly laid out lots. If the lot on the plan was painted yellow, the home was completed and occupied—42 of those so far. If it was green, the house had been started but was still unfinished; there were 68 green rectangles. As we looked around, we realized that the entire village was spruced up as we had never seen it before, with the grass neatly cut and the dirt paths cleared of weeds. A great deal of effort had gone into the preparations for this celebration.

Our evening consisted of a huge songfest in the village church, featuring vocal ensembles from all around Lake Tumba. So many people came that scores had to stand around outside the open-sided building, listening as group after group performed, each trying to outdo the previous one in their expressions of praise and joy. The five-part program went on till nearly midnight.

The next morning the first rooster had barely begun to announce the dawn when we heard outside our window more voices blended in song. The women of the village had returned to sing us awake!

The long-awaited dedication day officially began at 7 A.M. with a baptismal service at Lake Tumba. Nine pastors and evangelists waded out into the lake to a waist-high depth, and then the people walked out toward them, nine at a time. A total of 105 people of all ages professed their faith through immersion in this beautiful lake. It was just past sunrise. My heart was full as I watched this moving ceremony, and I realized there could not have been a more appropriate way to begin this important day.

With typical African timing, the dedication service scheduled for 10 A.M. got under way shortly after noon. Actually, we had to wait for more truck travelers like ourselves—church officials, government dignitaries, volunteers from other building projects, and even a choir of church women from the capital city of Kinshasa, who had somehow raised enough money to make this 500-mile trip. Hundreds of people from other towns around the sixty-mile-long lake had also paddled dugout canoes or walked great distances to share in this occasion. And at one side of the crowd, looking a little out of place in a village that had never known electricity or running water, were the cameras and sound equipment of a representative from Zaire National Television!

Neckties are forbidden for citizens of Zaire—they are vestiges of Western colonialism. But because neckties indicate proper and respectful attire on American men, Geoff and I were expected to wear them. We did—even though it was the hottest day we had encountered on this latest visit to Africa, and the service, held outdoors in one of the town's new parks, lasted four and a half hours. Occasionally some of the participants, local men dressed in traditional skins and feathers and carrying arrows and spears, would abruptly break into the proceedings and race around making fearsome noises to calm the fidgeting of restless children.

Despite the discomforts of the steamy tropical sun, the

excitement carried us all along. The service began with a rousing chorus of Zaire's national anthem. I brought personal words of encouragement, and enthusiastic messages were read from former volunteers, missionaries, and supporters in the United States, Canada, and Germany; forty-two Bibles were given to the families whose homes had been completed; there were lengthy greetings from church and government leaders who were present; there were scripture readings and familiar hymns, simultaneously sung in English, French, and Lingala, the local tongue (you could take your pick); there was a spellbinding speech by Sam Mompongo and an inspiring sermon by the national president of the Protestant Church in Zaire; and there were gifts and offerings to be presented and received, including $2,000 for another house from Geoff's church in California, with a pledge of $2,000 more within the next three months—and what a roar of approval greeted that announcement!

Finally the long service drew to a close, and we all stood for a prayer of benediction. By that time everyone was sweaty and tired, and the uncomprehending children were thoroughly exhausted. Suddenly something happened which grabbed the attention of the entire multitude. Discomfort was forgotten, and total silence descended on 3,000 people, as the Ntondo choir stepped forward and began to sing, in perfect harmony, the "Hallelujah Chorus" from Handel's *Messiah.*

They must have rehearsed for months. The language was Lingala, but this musical explosion of praise and thanksgiving to God would have been understandable in any country on earth. And the experience of listening to Handel's immortal composition, sung as effectively in the hot sun of an equatorial jungle village as it might have been in a great European cathedral, was one I am not likely ever to forget.

In the hush that followed that final, exultant "Hallelujah!" I felt as if I might burst with joy. I thanked God fervently for bringing me to this occasion.

Suddenly I realized that, without my knowing it, my entire life's experiences had been gradually pointing me toward my present involvement in this exciting community-building effort. And even during the long years when I ignored Him almost completely, God had kept on nudging me, constantly providing indications of the direction He had for my life.

But it took a long while for me to decide to pay attention.

2

Home Repairs for Beginners

I especially remember another hot day, in the long-ago summer of 1945. My dad and I were bouncing happily down a red Alabama dirt lane in his ancient car. We had traveled about five miles off the main highway between Lanett and Lafayette (pronounced locally "la-FETT," so that the two names rhymed). I was ten years old and overflowing with excitement.

Only the day before, my dad had closed the deal on a 400-acre farm at the end of this road, and I was enjoying visions of roaming through endless unexplored territory. The woods and hedgerows, I was sure, were bound to be populated with rabbits, possums, quail, and other game with which I would fill the family's larder.

Actually, the farm was not particularly promising. Some of the fields were swampy, and most of the rest were hilly and stony; there was only a small percentage of tillable land. Even the lumber had recently been cut off, by a work crew of German prisoners of war who were interned in a nearby camp. Apparently the farm's previous owners had decided there was little more cash to be made from the place, and they sold it to my dad, the proprietor of a Lanett grocery store, for $3.75 an acre. Even in 1945, for rather poor farmland, that price represented a considerable bargain.

The property was known locally as a "two-nigger farm." The first dilapidated shack we came to as we drove down the lane from the Lafayette highway was the home of elderly Bud Lancaster and his wife Mattie, alone since all their children had grown up and left. Just beyond, down a rocky hill, lived Macy Glaze and his family in another flimsy, unpainted shack.

Bud's first complaint to the farm's new owner, when he met my dad, was that the German prisoners were going into his cornfield and eating the ears raw! But the POWs left when we took possession, so Bud and Macy turned our attention to their next pressing problem—the rundown houses. At the same time, Bud pointed out that the walls of the well had recently caved in and that there was precious little water in it.

My dad was a compassionate man, and he listened with concern as Bud and Macy appealed for better living quarters. But my father was far from wealthy, and there were limits to what he could afford to do. After surveying both situations carefully, he decided to do rather extensive work on Bud's house and to dig him a new well. Macy's shack, he felt, was too far gone to justify more than minor repairs. Macy was unhappy about this, and a few months later he and his family simply left. I never found out where they went. But within a year, his old house completely collapsed.

Meanwhile, we set to work on Bud's house. It had no ceilings; the interior walls were simply the backs of the planks which formed the outside walls. The ancient roof was full of holes. On rainy days there weren't enough buckets to catch the drips, and on sunny days streams of light came through to pattern the floors—which were also full of holes.

The house was a battered rectangular box consisting of two rooms and a center hall. There was a front door for coming and going, and a back door for tossing out dishwater and spitting snuff juice. It would be a major job to put this dwelling into decent shape, but I was eager to get started. I was embarking on an adventure. Bud and I were to do most of the work, with help from my dad whenever he was available.

We began by shoring up the foundation with new columns of concrete blocks. When we had succeeded in banging some blocks in under the house, we'd go indoors and jump up and down to see whether the floor still shook; if it did, we pounded in more blocks. We followed this procedure until the rickety old shack had become rock-solid underneath. Next, we ripped off the tattered roof, put on new decking, and rolled out fresh, bright-green roofing. Finally, we nailed on artificial red-brick siding. It was an asphalt material with fake bricks that wouldn't fool anybody, but this covering would keep out at least some of the winter wind.

For the inside, my dad obtained some huge plywood boxes that had been packing cases for coffins, and we used this wood for ceilings and walls in both rooms and the hallway. When we had patched the holes in the floor, we painted the entire inside of the house an electric pink color. Bud and Mattie were ecstatic; they had never lived in anything so beautiful as this colorful, coffin-carton house. And I discovered, to my delight, that their joy was also a personal thrill to me.

Once the old house was refurbished, we were ready to work on the well. All during the time we were repairing his home, Bud kept talking about going out into the woods for just the right forked stick. With the aid of this indispensable tool he would locate the spot where we should dig. "Dowsing" may not be the scientifically approved method for finding water everywhere, but it was common practice in our part of rural Alabama.

"When I walk around with that stick in my hand," he would explain excitedly, "that ole stick gonna just flip down and point right toward the ground. And that's where we'll dig—cause that's where the vein of water be."

When the important day arrived, we drove out to Bud's house early in the morning, along with a couple of extra fellows to help dig. We had brought heavy ropes, picks, shovels, buckets, and a winch for winding the rope and bucket up out of the hole. Bud was out front waiting for us, holding that perfect Y-shaped stick carefully in his hand.

"You ready?" he asked, flashing a big toothless grin. He had just two teeth in his mouth, and only a few fuzzy gray hairs still clung around the edges of his otherwise bald head.

"Yes, Bud," my dad replied. "Tell us where to dig!"

Immediately Bud squashed a wrinkled work cap down on his head and became thoroughly serious. "Come on," he said. "Let's get busy."

We followed obediently around to the back of the house. At the corner of the building Bud bent over, heisted up his pant legs, and very carefully grasped one side of the V of the forked stick in each hand. He aimed the point of the branch straight ahead of him, about a foot above the ground, and began to creep along in this half-crouch with the most solemn look that I had ever seen on his face. Slowly and deliberately he progressed to the back corner of his yard, as all of us watched intently in absolute silence. Nothing happened. Then he gradually turned and came back, still at a turtle's pace, this time heading diagonally toward the center of the house. About halfway back he stopped abruptly. The forked stick was trembling; then it began, slowly at first and then more definitely, to point down toward the earth.

"Here!" Bud's voice exploded the stillness. "I think the water's here!

He marked a big X on the spot with the heel of his boot, and then hurried to the opposite corner of the house. Carefully following his previous routine—mash down the hat, pull up the trousers, grasp the stick, scrunch over, and proceed silently—he crept across the yard again, toward his X. His expression, more grave than ever, added to the tension among the spectators. As he neared the marked area, I simply quit breathing. Suddenly the forked stick began to quiver again, and gradually it veered down until it was clearly pointing toward exactly the same spot as before.

"This is it. This is it!" he yelled. "It's a big vein. The pull is real strong. Ain't no question about it."

Bud made the X deeper with his heavy boot and then stepped back, lifted his cap and proudly wiped the sweat from his forehead. He was beaming.

My dad accepted Bud's decision. Looking around at us, he commanded, "Let's get busy, boys!"

I don't remember how many days it took to dig that well, but it seemed an incredibly long task. I do remember that we hit rock about thirty feet down and that we had to get dynamite to blast through. That part was exciting: drilling holes in the rock, packing in sticks of dynamite, and carefully placing the caps to set it off; attaching the wires and then climbing out of the hole to touch the wire ends to the car battery; hearing a huge THUD and feeling the earth shake under us.

After each blast I would climb back down into the hole to gather rock fragments, packing them into the bucket and yelling up, "Take it away!" My pleasure at being an important participant in this activity was compounded by the thrill of danger that accompanied working down inside that well—especially after we hit water. As the buckets full of mud and rocks whirled on the way up, occasionally banging against the sides of the hole and spilling debris back onto my head, I always wondered what it would be like if the rope broke, or the winch snapped, or the person pulling that bucket thirty or forty feet above me lost his grip.

Fortunately, we all survived. Furthermore, Bud and Mattie got plenty of good clear water to go with their rejuvenated house. They were overjoyed with what had been accomplished, and so was I.

What I didn't understand then, or for a long time thereafter, was that this experience of repairing a house and digging a well was just one of many that God would use to train me for the job He had in store for me. At the age of ten, I had found out how to lay one block on top of another. But it was not until many years later that I learned to put *love* in the mortar joints.

3
A Profitable Partnership

Over the next fifteen years I had many more opportunities to learn about building and repairing houses. At no time, however, was I interested in doing this in order to assist anyone else. My object was simply to make money.

During the summer of 1955, while I was a student at Auburn University in Auburn, Alabama, I spent my vacation working on a construction crew in Flint, Michigan. I mixed mortar, poured foundations, laid blocks, and did all kinds of carpentry. At this job I made just about enough money so that by the end of August I was able to purchase a rattletrap secondhand Ford. Trailing clouds of smoke, burning nearly a quart of oil for each tank of gasoline, I drove triumphantly back to Auburn for the fall quarter.

A couple of years later I was a law student at the University of Alabama in Tuscaloosa. A fellow student, Morris Dees, and I formed a business partnership, and one of the enterprises we decided to try was investing in real estate. That is, we would purchase or lease some dilapidated housing near the campus, clean and remodel the buildings, and rent rooms and apartments to students.

Of course, we first needed some working capital. To acquire that, we tackled a great many other enterprises. We tried selling mistletoe and cypress knees; both efforts were financial disasters. We also peddled holly wreaths, Christmas decorations, rubber doormats, and student telephone directories, and these projects began to turn a welcome profit. We were both determined financial adventurers, and we would try any crazy idea that looked potentially rewarding.

Over the years we used at least a dozen different business names; if a new product or idea did not seem to fit into an existing company, we just thought up another one. Fuller and Dees Heart of Dixie Products, Home Ec Press, Athletic Publishing Company, and Off to College, Inc., were just a few of our ventures.

At one point in our student-directory sales program we uncovered the interesting information that approximately sixteen students on the campus had a birthday every day. Immediately another of our enterprises was born—the Bama Cake Service.

At the beginning of each school year, postcards for all parents were addressed and stacked in chronological order according to the birth dates of the students. These cards were carefully mailed each day to parents of students whose birthdays were two weeks hence, inviting the parents to order a birthday cake and have it personally delivered by a representative of the Bama Cake Service. By contracting with a local baker, we sold four or more cakes a day for three years—with an average profit of $2 per cake. And this required a daily investment of half an hour of delivery time by Morris or myself!

Another enterprise that we undertook was selling advertising on large, desk-size blotters to merchants near several college campuses. These heavy desk pads, which included sports schedules and dormitory phone numbers, were then distributed free to students. Our profit came from the ads placed by local businesses.

One afternoon I was pounding the pavements in Tuscaloosa, selling advertising. I had no inkling that this would be one of the most important days of my life. I stopped at a movie theater and asked for the manager, and while I waited for someone to fetch him, I chatted with the girl in the ticket window. She was attractive and friendly—and just as I was about to ask for her phone number, the manager appeared.

By the time I had gone into his office and signed him up for an ad and returned to the front of the theater, the shift had changed. The pretty young ticket seller was gone.

"Where is Joan?" I asked. At least I had learned that much.

"She's gone home. She's through working for today."

"What's her telephone number?"

"We aren't allowed to give out that information."

"What's her address?"

"We can't give out that information either."

I was becoming exasperated. I wanted to talk to that girl again!

"Please let me speak to the manager."

Again someone was sent to fetch him. When he returned, I explained my problem, thinking that surely he would be sympathetic.

He wasn't. Not at all.

"I can't give out that information. No, sir!"

That was that.

By this time my mind was totally off the business of selling ads and totally on that girl. I decided what I would do. I was pretty sure that she had said her last name was Caldwell. I would simply go back to my room and phone all the Caldwells in the Tuscaloosa telephone book if necessary. Somehow, I would get to talk to her today!

The first number I called produced a pleasant-sounding girl. Success so quickly!

"No, I'm not Joan."

"Do you know Joan Caldwell?"

"No."

"Thank you."

The second number also produced a girl. Success for sure!

"No, I'm not Joan."

"Do you know her?"

"No."

"Thank you."

The third number produced yet another girl! This *had* to be the right one.

"No, I'm not Joan."

I explained my problem. I had met Joan at the box office of the theater, and now I was trying to locate her.

This girl was sympathetic, and she really tried to be helpful. She offered first one suggestion and then another. As she talked, I began to lose interest in Joan—this girl sounded *so* nice over the phone.

Finally I could contain my curiosity no longer.

"What's *your* name?" I blurted out.

"Linda."

We continued chatting, discovering in the process that we had several mutual friends. Joan receded farther and farther into the background. Suddenly Linda asked how tall I was.

"I'm six feet four inches."

"Well, I'm five feet ten inches!"

I could tell by the tone of her voice that she was now much more interested in me. I asked if I could come out to meet her. She said yes, and began giving me directions.

In a few minutes I was knocking on Linda Caldwell's door. Shortly thereafter we were in the Student Union Cafeteria of the University of Alabama, having a snack and getting better acquainted.

A year later, in August of 1959, this beautiful young lady became my wife.

(Long before that, however, Linda was hard at work for Fuller and Dees enterprises. As a matter of fact, she has reminded me since that she was so busy typing envelopes for one of our big promotional mailings that she couldn't fit in time to shampoo her hair the day before our wedding!)

As the first profits gradually accumulated from the variety of ventures that Morris and I undertook, the money went straight into real estate holdings. We began by leasing a rundown six-room house near the campus, fixing it up ourselves and subleasing rooms. I was still single at that point, and I moved into one room to manage the house.

Then we leased the backyard to two house trailers. By this time our income on the property was more than double our rental expense.

Next, we went to the other end of the block and purchased a four-unit apartment building, and then an adjacent two-story house, which we promptly renovated and turned into four more apartments. Now we found ourselves spending evenings, weekends, and all our holidays painting, plumbing, and repairing, along with cleaning up yards and planting shrubbery.

Our final acquisition was a vacant lot situated between the apartment houses and the rooming house. This gave us control of the entire side of that street from one avenue to the other. For the empty lot, we were able to purchase a former army barracks, which was brought to the site by a professional house mover. With the help of my dad, who came to Tuscaloosa for a week to work with us, we cleaned up that old box and converted it into three more student apartments.

When this fourth building was completed, forty-some students were renting rooms, apartments, or trailer space from us, and we took in between $800 and $1,000 per month in rent. Of course, we also experienced the headaches that come with being landlords. Like the night some students who were celebrating a bit too much chopped three doors off their hinges, piled up the wood in a huge bonfire, and went into a wild "Indian dance" around it. *Indoors!*

In spite of some real problems, during 1959, my last year of law school, my partner and I grossed almost $20,000 from real estate rentals, followed by the sale of the properties. Our other enterprises earned us $30,000 more. As the end of our university careers approached, we were making plans for the opening of our new office in Montgomery, and for branching out into more business deals on the side. Morris and I already had a pocketful of money, but we were sure there were a lot more exciting times ahead.

I just didn't have any idea *how* exciting.

4
Making Money in Montgomery

Montgomery—the cradle of the Confederacy, the capital city of Alabama. And in 1960, the new home of Dees and Fuller, Attorneys at Law, and Fuller & Dees, Inc., business enterprises.

We had agreed upon Montgomery as the home of our law practice and expanding business ventures because it was a large city with good mail and transportation connections, and because Morris Dees had many contacts in the area since it was near his home. In addition, both of us had developed an interest in politics, and Montgomery was the political center of the state.

However, thanks to our growing business, our law practice would last less than two years, and our interest in politics would gradually dwindle. But Fuller & Dees, Inc., and our related ventures would really mushroom in the months ahead. Many of our enterprises at college—the Bama Cake Service, student telephone directories, desk pads, student apartments—had already been terminated because they were strictly campus activities, but the direct mail operation selling holly wreaths and doormats for fund raising was continued.

And we began to seek other products to be sold by mail to groups wishing to earn money.

Before long, we were promoting locally produced tractor cushions as fundraisers for all the high school Future Farmers of America chapters in the United States. We ended up selling 100,000 cushions—when the most the company could make by our delivery deadline, working seven days a week around the clock, was 65,000! But even after having to refuse a third of our orders, we showed a net profit of close to $75,000.

Then we got into cookbooks of favorite recipes of America's home economics teachers, to be sold by the Future Homemakers of America. The project was an incredible success, and we soon branched out into dozens of other titles, like *Recipes on Parade* (favorite recipes of military officers' wives), *A Lion in the Kitchen* (for Lions Clubs), and *Favorite Recipes of the Deep South* (and of New England, the Eastern Star, and Pilot Clubs). We even made up a cookbook called *My Favorite Recipes,* which sold thousands—and there was nothing in it but chapter headings and blank pages to be filled in by the owner! Within two years we were the largest publisher of cookbooks in the nation. Other money-makers we printed included a national directory of high school coaches, a series of Junior Achievement yearbooks, and a magazine for students called *Off to College.*

As our businesses grew, we kept hiring more people and moving into larger and fancier quarters. Fuller & Dees, Inc., had begun in 1960 in our law office, which consisted of three small rented rooms and one employee. By late 1963, we had to send a panel truck to the post office every day to pick up the mail, and we had moved into a modern, spacious office building on the edge of Montgomery, for which we paid $100,000 cash. I also remember 1963 as the first year our company sold a million toothbrushes, and the year we grossed a million dollars for the first time.

In January of 1964 I wrote in my personal journal:

> Sales for last year exceeded a million dollars! We set this goal long ago and we finally made it. Now we want ten million! And we'll make it within six years, with a little luck. . . .

Of course, as the company grew, so did my personal affluence. During our early days in business together, my partner and I owned a secondhand panel truck between us, in which we delivered everything from Christmas trees to birthday cakes. It was also the only transportation Linda and I had for dates. Since there was just one single seat, she had to sit precariously beside me on an apple crate, and our handholding was as much for reasons of necessity as for romance! We did get a car of our own shortly after our marriage in 1959. However, it had no heater, and there were so many rusted holes in the floorboard that in winter we seldom traveled more than a few blocks in it—we couldn't stand the cold wind. When I graduated from law school in 1960, we traded in this old hulk for a newer, but still secondhand, bright-green Chevrolet. The next year it was a new Ford, and then came a fancier Buick. By 1964, Morris and I were able to go downtown together, pick out a Lincoln Continental with all the luxury options for each of us—elegant gray for me, glossy black for him—and pay cash for both cars on the spot.

Over the same span of time our family's living accommodations had gone from a two-room student apartment to an eight-room house in Montgomery, which we remodeled extensively and filled with expensive furniture, carpets, wallpaper, and drapes. But before long we wanted a bigger, more impressive dwelling, so we purchased twenty acres in an exclusive area east of the city. A prominent architect drew us a plan for a gorgeous new home, a barn and pasture for saddle horses, and of course a swimming pool.

We were already keeping saddle horses out in the country on our three cattle farms that totaled some 2,000 acres. Linda and I also had a cabin on Lake Jordan, near Montgomery, two speedboats, and a full-time maid to help with the children, Chris and Kim. Linda had so many clothes and shoes that she had a constant problem finding closet space—and we had *lots* of closets!

Morris Dees and I, from the first day of our partnership, shared one overriding purpose: to make a pile of money. We were not particular about *how* we did it; we just wanted to be independently rich. During the eight years that we worked together, we never wavered in that resolve. And when the treasurer of our company walked into my office one day in 1964 to inform me that I was worth a million dollars, it came as no great surprise. I accepted her report with satisfaction and turned immediately to my next goal: *ten* million dollars.

But everything has a price. And I paid for our success in several ways.

One price I paid was estrangement from the church.

From earliest childhood I had been brought up in the church, and I believed in the Christian message. As a teenager, I was president of the youth organization of the Southeast Conference of Congregational Christian Churches (now the United Church of Christ), and I traveled around six states in this capacity.

While I was at the university, I temporarily abandoned the church. Occasionally I would attend with Linda, but my reasons for going were not really worshipful ones!

When we settled in Montgomery, I returned to active participation in the church, and in fact Linda and I organized a new United Church of Christ in our home. Again, I was persuaded to accept an office of leadership in the Southeast Conference. Nevertheless, I was still giving only the leftovers of my time to the Lord. If anything in my business conflicted with church activities, the business always came first. I wanted to serve God through the church, but at my own convenience, and without any interference with my financial enterprises.

What my real priorities were in those days became very clear after one crucial decision I made. On July 30, 1964, I received an unexpected letter from the National Stewardship Council of the United Church of Christ, asking me to visit overseas missionaries. The Council requested that I spend several weeks touring areas where the denomination had mission work; upon my return, I would be expected to give some time speaking to churches, conferences, and other religious gatherings, sharing what I had seen and learned on my trip.

My first impulse, after reading this unexpected invitation, was to accept. This was an assignment that I could do, and it was something I would enjoy. Furthermore, it was a task that needed to be done, because so many of our congregations knew little about the mission of the church beyond their own communities. Deep within me, I knew I should go. The invitation seemed a call from God to perform a unique service for Him.

But I began to toss other questions around in my mind. "What will this trip cost me?" I was not concerned about plane tickets, lodging, or meals—I could pay that easily. My larger concern was the cost of being away from our booming company. What would such a trip, and the expected speaking engagements afterward, mean in terms of lost income from "neglecting" the company? I scribbled some figures on a note pad. The cost was too high. I called in a secretary and quickly dictated a letter declining the invitation.

When she had left, I recall pushing my chair back from the desk and reflecting awhile. There was a deep sadness within me because I knew God had knocked at my door and I had turned Him away. "Oh, well," I reasoned, "I'll probably do it later. Now is not a convenient time." I *had* written, in declining the invitation, "I'll go in two years, perhaps."

I have come to know, in later years, that God often calls us into service at what we consider the most inopportune time. And how often we point this out to Him! "No, Lord," we complain, "not now. Not today. Not this week. Not this year." Or more often, "Not me, now or ever. Somebody else would be better."

One day Jesus asked a couple of men to follow him. "Sir," one of them replied, "first let me go and bury my father." The other man said, "First let me go and say good-bye to my family." Jesus answered the first man, "Let the dead bury their own dead. You go and preach the Kingdom of God." He told the second man, "Anyone who starts to plow and then keeps looking back is of no use to the Kingdom of God."[1]

A few months after my partner and I had launched our

company back at the University of Alabama, I bowed my head in my room one night and promised the Lord I would always seek His Kingdom first in my life, regardless of the success or failure of the business. But as time went along, more and more frequently I was saying no to God and yes to business deals and personal wealth. Clearly, in declining the invitation to visit missionaries, I put the work of the Kingdom solidly in second place.

In our local congregation, I was quite happy when our new church called its first pastor. He would relieve me of much of the work, I thought. However, that was not the case. He wanted me to get busier than ever! Calls on prospective members should be made; the purchase of land ought to be concluded as soon as possible; more Sunday school teachers must be recruited; and a dozen other needs were pressing.

I recall clearly that I used to grimace when the receptionist at the office would buzz my phone to tell me the preacher was out front. What now? I didn't want to see him. I hated the thought of doing more church work. I was busy; why couldn't *he* take care of the church?

Jesus spoke a clear warning about this attitude. "No one can be a slave to two masters. He will hate one and love the other; he will be loyal to one and despise the other. You cannot serve both God and Money."[2]

I kept trying to serve both. God was to be God, but money would also be God. In truth, I came to hate the church and the meetings and all the demands made on me. I hated all that went with keeping up my "image" as a Christian businessman.

Actually, my main reason for working with the church was to create this impression of myself among friends and associates. In many sections of the United States, and especially in the South, it is important financially to appear to be a Christian. The successful, wholesome young man is active in his church. So for my own credit and praise I wanted the correct image, but I wanted to acquire it in my spare time—not at the expense of the company or my personal pleasure.

Not only did the church receive the leftover crumbs of my time and interest; it also got only the crumbs of my money.

When I made $60,000 a year in salary, I gave the church $40 a month; after my salary increased to $100,000 a year, I gave $80. I rationalized this tiny offering on the theory that a larger one would wreck the budget of the church! But I didn't contribute anything to other Christian agencies either.

In our age of unprecedented prosperity, people in the middle and upper classes of our society should give *more* than the Biblical 10 percent to churches and to voluntary agencies that are concerned with ministering to the physical and spiritual needs of people. Certainly I could have been giving much more, but instead I gave less—less than 1 percent! Years earlier, when I made only a fraction of $100,000 a year, I gave 10 percent, and more, to the church. As I became more affluent, however, I constantly decreased the percentage of giving. A tenth of $100,000 is $10,000. That was just too much to give away! "I'll keep the money now," I reasoned, "so I'll have more to give later."

Another high price I paid for my personal affluence was a compromising of my personal morality and integrity.

Back at the university, when my partner and I needed lumber for repairs on our apartment houses, I went to the buildings and grounds supervisor and got permission to take a *few* pieces of *old* lumber. When he left, and no one was looking, I would take all we needed, new and used alike. And although we were always honest and fair with our customers—that was good business—with suppliers it was frequently another story. For instance, I once wrote up a contract with a printing company promising to buy from them for a period of years at a specified price. Knowing they intended to purchase equipment especially for our work, I deliberately "fixed" the contract so it could be broken if we were able to get a better price from another printer before the contract term expired. If we secured a lower bid, we would then be in a position to force the company with whom we had the contract to reduce their price still farther, in order to salvage their huge investment in new equipment.

During the election campaign of 1958, while I was still at the university, I became West Alabama campaign manager for McDonald Gallion, who was then running for state attorney general. Morris dropped out of school for one semester to serve as state campaign manager. We wanted to be sure of having friends in high places when we arrived in Montgomery a couple of years later.

Even though by that time I no longer believed in racial discrimination, I spoke to all-white groups more than seventy times during that campaign, and in every speech I preached segregation. One of my speeches was in Fayette, Alabama, to a huge gathering of robed Klansmen. The meeting was held in the county courthouse in the middle of town. So many Klansmen had gathered that night that they could not all get inside the building. A public address system was rigged up so those outside could hear, and my rousing preachments against black people were boomed out over several city blocks.

Of course, my political speeches in those meetings were not inconsistent with what I had been taught in my church back in Lanett, Alabama. As a boy in Sunday school, I recall lessons about prejudice and discrimination, but the examples given described Indians being mistreated in New Mexico, or Japanese and Mexicans in California. There was never a word about blacks in Alabama. Blacks were inferior; they should be kept segregated and in their place. I had been carefully brought up to believe that.

I first began to question this idea at Christian youth conferences I attended as a teenager. In those meetings, at Elmhurst College in Illinois, Catawba College in North Carolina, Doane College in Nebraska, and Yale University in Connecticut, I had my first opportunties to meet and work with blacks as equals. Suddenly, in the light of the New Testament, I began to see clearly the terrible wrongs in the social system of my native South.

But my burning ambition to succeed kept pushing this enlightenment into the background. I had to keep it covered up; it would be bad for business if rising young lawyers and businessmen spoke out for social justice and equality.

In 1961, a few months after we had arrived in Montgomery, some Freedom Riders came to town. Prior to that time, black people had always had to sit at the back of interstate buses in the South, and were forced to use segregated restrooms and denied service at bus terminal lunch counters. Congress had already passed legislation outlawing these forms of discrimination, but the practice remained. The Freedom Riders, an integrated group, traveled from city to city putting this legislation to a practical test. All morning on May 21, 1961, the local radio station blared the news of the impending arrival of these "integrationists" at the Montgomery bus station. Since our office was only a few blocks from the station, I walked down there to witness the riders' reception. It was a sad spectacle.

I wrote about it the next day in my diary.

> The integrated "Freedom Riders" came into town on a Greyhound bus yesterday. They were met at the station by a mob, and two of the group were severely beaten. Newsmen and cameramen were also attacked and beaten. The police did not show up until twenty-five or thirty minutes after the violence had erupted. When they finally came, they made no real effort to stop the brutality. Later in the day, when the mob could not find the Freedom Riders, they turned on innocent Negroes who were just standing around looking. They beat one old crippled Negro man. I think the action of this mob is senseless and utterly crazy, and the action by the governor, the sheriff, and the police department is inexcusable. They could have, and should have, been present to prevent this violence. . . .

I could express my true sentiments in the diary. It was private. But when one of the men charged with beating the Freedom Riders came to our law office for legal representation, we took the case. Our fee was paid by the Klan and the White Citizens' Council. We expressed openly our sympathies and support for what had happened at the bus station!

(Two years later, we did begin to indicate publicly our feelings about equal treatment and opportunities for blacks. For example, our company hired a black to head our in-plant printing department, the first black person in the city to hold such a position. The following summer we recruited thirteen black high school and college students to package sample products for the fall mailings. That Christmas we held a company party at the big Jeff Davis Hotel in downtown Montgomery, and all employees were invited, black and white. We were the first company in the city to hold an integrated party. There was a certain personal risk in such initiatives, but practically none financially. By this time we were out of the law practice, and our local business was infinitesimal in volume compared with the national totals. We could afford to be at least a little moral.)

Estrangement from the church, personal immorality in various forms, compromise with principle—all these were part of the price I was paying for success. But there was another big payment, too. I was losing my health.

On April 8, 1964, I wrote about this problem in my diary.

> My neck has been hurting for a week. I would like to know what is the matter with it. I haven't been well for three weeks. First my kidneys got out of whack; then I had headaches. My neck started hurting. About four days ago my back ached miserably. Now my neck hurts again. I'll be glad to get back into one hundred percent good health!

Shortly thereafter, I developed a severe breathing problem. Often my chest felt as if tremendous pressure were bearing down on it. I gasped for breath. Hundreds of times I grabbed hold of the arms of my office chair and struggled to fill my lungs with air. Often I had to leave my desk and walk around the office or even around the building in order to relax enough to resume normal breathing.

A few people saw what was happening to me. My father issued a warning several times, and others dropped hints that I might be heading for bigger trouble.

Donald Moore, a cousin with whom I had sold mistletoe back at Auburn, came to my office one day and asked me to step outside with him. We walked out on the manicured lawn in front of the building. He stooped down, pulled off a blade of grass and started chewing on it. I squatted beside him.

"What is it, Donald?" I inquired.

"I don't know how to say this, Millard," he started, "but I think you're off on the wrong track. Haven't your values gotten out of perspective in the process of building up this business?"

I looked him straight in the eye and laughed. He was right, but I was not ready to admit it.

The business was a fantastic success. I should have been pleased and happy; instead, I was anxious, depressed, and nervous. I felt something was wrong, but I couldn't afford to change anything. I had too much to lose. I continued working long hours and struggling to breathe. My health problems, I told myself, were simply part of the price I had to pay for success. My breathing, and everything else, would soon return to normal.

I kept pushing.

Perhaps one of my varied maladies would shortly have killed me; I don't know. But Linda precipitated a crisis first. In November 1965, she left me. Our love relationship had cooled to the point that about the only thing we still shared was our king-size bed, and now I was going to lose her.

This, I discovered, was the price I was not willing to pay. My father had lost his wife, my mother, when she was only twenty-four, and I was three. Her sudden death was shattering to my dad. As I grew up, he frequently told me about my mother, and how much he loved her and what a wonderful person she was. I cried often as a boy because my mother had died so young and I never got to know her. I recall that even then I prayed that God would guide me to a very special wife and that He would spare me the agony of losing her.

When I met Linda that afternoon in Tuscaloosa, I was absolutely captivated. I was sure from the first day I saw her that this was the girl I wanted to marry. And our wedding on August 30, 1959, was the happiest occasion of my life.

But even though I loved Linda deeply, as time went along, I neglected her more and more. The business increasingly took first place in my life, ahead of everything else, Linda included. This was especially true after we moved to Montgomery. Rarely did we have private time together—I was always too busy.

My partner and his wife lived out in the country; we lived

in town. Practically every morning he would come in to our house and sit with us as we were having breakfast. He and I talked business while Linda listened, or pretended to. I did not come home for lunch. At night, either he and I came to our house to eat supper, and again to talk business while Linda listened, or we simply stayed in town and ate at a restaurant. Often I did not get home before midnight. This went on for years.

Only after our marriage had nearly ended in divorce did I realize how insensitive I had been toward Linda in those early years. When we moved to Montgomery, she was only nineteen, and our son Chris, who was born in July 1960, was two months old. I soon bought a big, fancy house in an exclusive section of town where she was surrounded by people twenty to fifty years older than she was, and there I virtually abandoned her, except in the middle of the night! She would tell me of salesmen coming to our door during the day; when she answered their ring, they would ask if her mother was home! We both laughed about it. To me it was really funny, and I was pleased to have a pretty young wife, securely ensconced in an impressive house. But to Linda it was not funny at all. Many nights, she confided later, she would drive to a nearby shopping center and push Chris around in his stroller until she was exhausted enough to sleep. She was so lonely she couldn't stand it.

I will never forget the Saturday night in November 1965, when I came home from the office, late as always. Linda was waiting up for me, sitting on the side of our bed. Immediately I could tell something was seriously bothering her. She fiddled with her fingers for a couple of minutes and gazed down at her lap.

"What's the matter, Sweetheart?"

She looked up suddenly, right into my face. "How do you know you love me?" Her face was ashen, the corners of her mouth twitching.

"I just love you, that's all. I love everything about you. I . . ."

She didn't let me finish.

"I'm going away for a while," she said. "I don't know if

we've got a future together or not. I want to think over a lot of things."

I was speechless. Linda had come to my office a year and a half earlier to announce that she didn't love me anymore. I had been shocked by that, but not shocked enough to do anything about it. I continued to work from early in the morning until late at night. We rarely had any time together, but I thought she had accepted that. After all, she had been attending nearby Huntingdon College and was extremely busy herself. She had completed requirements for her college degree in August, and I believed we were on the way to recovering the spark in our marriage.

Until this moment.

I tried vainly to dissuade her. She had to talk to someone, she said, and then she added, "I don't want to hang out our dirty linen here in Montgomery." She told me that she had decided to go to New York to talk with Dr. Lawrence Durgin, pastor of the Broadway United Church of Christ. We both knew Dr. Durgin from a brief stay in New York a couple of years earlier, when we had attended his church three or four times.

On Sunday, the day after her announcement, Linda drove to the airport in her car and caught a plane to New York. In my car, the children—Chris, then five, and Kim, three—and I went out to one of our farms. I had a lot of thinking to do myself.

The long week that followed was the loneliest, most agonizing time of my life. When I went to my office, I couldn't stay in the room alone. Since I had wanted to review our company's projects with key personnel and plan sales strategy for the coming year, I arranged for all department heads to meet me on Lake Jordan at our cabin. We gathered there every day during that week, and I talked and talked and talked, trying to keep my mind off my tottering marriage. I did not breathe a word to anyone about my personal problems. It would be bad for the company to upset employees with my marital difficulties.

At five o'clock each afternoon—instead of my usual midnight—I went home to relieve our maid. I took Chris and Kim for walks. I tried to play with them, but my heart was not in it. I gave baths, searched drawers for clothes and pajamas, brushed teeth, and tucked sleepy children into bed. One evening, as I was pulling the blanket over Chris, he looked up at me in the dim light and said softly, "Daddy, I'm glad you're home."

Chills ran up my spine as I realized that I had indeed become a virtual stranger in my own house. Most mornings, I left for the office before the children awakened and came home after they had gone to sleep.

How had all this happened?

On the first night of our married life, Linda and I had signed an agreement in which we promised to "outlove" each other. We promised not to keep secrets and to maintain a right relationship with God. We had composed this covenant the week before our wedding, she writing one word and then handing me the pen to write the next. Then we had the document framed, and we hung it over our bed at every place we lived.

It was there now. During this week of sleepless nights I took down our agreement and reread it again and again. We had promised to outlove each other—and she was off in New York thinking about whether we had a future together, and I was in Montgomery feeling miserable and desperate.

Linda called on Thursday night and told me I could come to New York the following Tuesday. I wanted to go immediately, but she said no. She had planned more counseling sessions with Dr. Durgin, and she wanted more time to think.

I couldn't stay home any longer. I was about to go crazy. So I got a company pilot to rent a plane, and on Saturday, after leaving Chris and Kim with their grandparents, we flew off to Niagara Falls.

This plane trip began an incredible series of events in which God kept intervening in my life so clearly that the message was unmistakable.* By the time I got to New York on Tuesday, and Linda and I began our time of reconciliation, my momentous decision was already beginning to be

---

* See *Bokotola,* Chapter 1.

made. And when Linda agreed wholeheartedly, I knew it was absolutely right.

We would sell our land and houses and boats and cars and cattle and horses. We would also sell the business—to my partner if he wanted it, and to someone else if he didn't. *And we would give all the money away.*

We had gone too far down the wrong road to be able to correct our direction with a slight detour. We simply had to go back and start all over again, but this time we would let God choose the road for us.

As we began to do this, the love of Christ restored honesty to all our relationships. And our love for each other, which had nearly been lost, began gradually to return and to grow steadily stronger.

Together, Linda and I embarked on a tremendous journey of faith.

---

1. Luke 9:59-62.
2. Matthew 6:24.

5
Encounter at Koinonia Farm

When Linda and I made the decision to begin our lives over again under a new set of rules, we were in New York City. Within a few days we had returned to Montgomery, picked up Chris and Kim, and driven to Florida. We knew that we had to get away from everything, to think, to become reacquainted as a family—and most of all to seek new directions.

But when we headed back home from Florida, we still had not felt any clear indication of what we should do when we were no longer rich.

During our return trip to Montgomery, we stopped overnight in a motel in Albany, Georgia. At breakfast the next morning I remembered that Al and Carol Henry, longtime friends of ours, had recently moved to Koinonia Farm, a Christian community in Southwest Georgia. They had invited us to visit them. At that time, however, I had been so uninterested in anything called a "Christian community" that I now had no recollection of where Al had told me it was.

Now I decided to try to contact them. I asked Linda, but she couldn't remember the name of the town either.

I went to see whether Koinonia might be listed in the Albany phone directory. It wasn't. I dialed the information operator.

"Do you have a listing for Koinonia Farm?"

I could hear her flipping the pages.

"How do you spell it?"

"K-O-I-N—I'm not sure. Maybe C-O-I-N—."

"No, I don't find anything—."

"Thank you." I started to hang up. Just before the receiver cut us off, I heard her voice again. I put it back to my ear.

"Yes?"

"I think I know where it is."

"You do? Where?"

"I think it's near Americus."

"Where's that?"

"About forty miles north of Albany."

"Thank you."

I hung up, dialed the long-distance operator, and asked for Koinonia Farm in Americus. Within two minutes I was talking to my friend Al Henry.

"Hey, where are you, Millard?"

"We're here in Albany, and we'd like to come by for a short visit."

"Wonderful!" He proceeded to give me directions to the farm.

On the way to Koinonia, Linda and I decided that we would stay no more than a couple of hours, because they had not known we were coming and it would not be polite to be there at lunchtime.

Our plans didn't work out that way. Al and Carol insisted that we stay for lunch. They explained that everyone at Koinonia ate together at noon, in the community dining hall, and that there was always extra food.

As Al showed us around the farm, letting us all peer into barns and stroll through the delectable smells of the small pecan-shelling plant and the fruitcake- and candy-making shop, he gave us the history of the place. And he talked at length about Clarence Jordan, the spiritual leader of the community. He explained that Clarence and his wife Florence had founded Koinonia with another couple, Martin and Mabel England, back in 1942, just after Clarence had graduated from the Southern Baptist Seminary in Louisville with a Ph.D. in Greek New Testament. Members of the community had always sought to live a life of simplicity like that of the early Christians, sharing all things in common and practicing nonviolence. Clarence, who also held a degree in agriculture from the University of Georgia, had introduced a variety of new farming methods to the poor sharecroppers in the neighborhood. Blacks and whites worked and shared as equals at Koinonia, and irate whites in the area had responded with bombings, shootings, and beatings. Koinonia never retaliated. By noon, I was absolutely consumed with curiosity about this unusual community, and especially about this Clarence Jordan who took God's word so seriously and so literally.

When I first saw Clarence in the small community dining hall, I was disappointed. He looked so ordinary. A man in his mid-fifties with a ruddy complexion and a deeply tanned face and neck, he was wearing faded overalls and an old plaid shirt. Could this be the Greek scholar, the brilliant lecturer, the fearless opponent of racism and the Ku Klux Klan, that Al had been telling me about?

Koinonia had two other visitors that day besides our family. One was a retired Navy chaplain; the other was a reporter from the *Columbus* (Ga.) *Enquirer.* As we all sat on rickety fruit boxes and shared a simple but hearty meal, those two visitors fired questions at Clarence. His quiet answers were straightforward, often profound. When the meal ended, the other members of the community drifted out to return to their chores. But the two visitors remained, along with Clarence, Al, Linda, and me. They asked the questions, Clarence answered, and the rest of us listened.

As we sat there, enthralled by the spirit and keen insights of this great man of faith, it suddenly dawned on me that surely God had led us to this place. Only a week before, Linda and I had decided together to change completely the direction of our lives, but we hadn't known what to do next.

Now we had encountered a community of deeply committed Christians led by a man with the most penetrating understanding of the Bible I had ever heard, and a man who had the courage to act on this understanding. I realized with growing excitement that God had arranged for me to meet Clarence Jordan.

In order to test my instinctive feelings about this meeting, I began to share with Clarence and the others around the table the personal and spiritual crisis Linda and I had been going through, our decision to sell our interest in the company and to give the money away, and our determination to spend our lives in service to God's Kingdom.

Everyone listened intently as I poured out my story. They were all understanding and compassionate, but Clarence was especially so. His kind face, his earnest words of hope and encouragement, told me what I already knew in my heart. God had brought us together. My cup was running over!

When we had left the table, I spoke quietly to Linda. "I think God brought us here, Sweetheart. I think we should stay for a while."

She didn't hesitate. "I'm sure you're right. See if we can stay."

Clarence, along with Al and the others, quickly agreed. A little house in the center of the community compound was empty, and we could move in immediately. The farm was in the middle of the pecan season, and we could help out with packaging and shipping pecan orders. (Earlier, Koinonia had supported itself by raising produce and chickens, selling eggs, and running a roadside farm market, but in the late fifties the Ku Klux Klan had dynamited the roadside stand and slapped a boycott on the farm. The farm's local business had been totally destroyed. In order to survive, the community had launched a mail order business selling pecans and pecan products. Clarence, with his irrepressible sense of humor, inaugurated this enterprise with the advertising slogan, "Help us ship the nuts out of Georgia!")

During the month that followed (December 1965) I worked daily in the small shipping room with Clarence, packaging and mailing pecans, fruitcakes, and candy to customers all over the country. But frequently we would get so involved in talking about Jesus that all processing would stop. Both of us would put a foot up on the shipping table and talk about God's call to obedience, to following Christ in scorn of the consequences, to faithfulness and not to "successfulness." Clarence would remind me that many people wish to deify Jesus and to worship Him, but they do not want to obey Him.

"Clarence," I said one day, "I feel a bit guilty about my work here with you. Actually, I'm more of a hindrance. You have so many orders to get out, and all I do is bother you with questions about theology."

He looked me squarely in the eye. "Millard," he replied, "you owe me no apologies. People are more important than pecans! The Lord's work is first; the pecans come second."

Koinonia had one old milk cow, and Clarence was the chief milker. Since I had had experience milking cows after my dad bought that farm near Lanett, I signed on as Clarence's assistant. I wanted to take advantage of every possible opportunity to talk to him. So each morning and evening we would march off to the little cow barn together and he would sit down on one side of the stall and I would sit on the other. He would get two teats and I would get two. We would squirt milk into the bucket and talk about Jesus as we peered at each other between the cow's tail and her hind legs. Fortunately, the Koinonia cow also practiced gentleness and nonviolence!

In the evenings we would frequently sit around in the Jordans' apartment, munching popcorn and peanuts from the farm, and talk still more about Christ and what it means to be His disciple in our modern world. At that time Clarence was in the process of translating portions of the New Testament into his "Cotton Patch" versions,* and he would often read to us what he had worked on that day to see if the meaning was clear. His purpose, he said, was to translate the scriptures in such a way that people in South Georgia would see Jesus and His message come alive in their locality, in their day.

---

* These versions were published in a series of four books between 1968 and 1973 by Association Press.

In Clarence's translation, Atlanta was Jerusalem. Valdosta was Bethlehem, and the road from Jerusalem to Jericho started in Atlanta and ended in Albany. The man who fell among thieves experienced that misfortune in Ellaville. A white revival preacher went by on the other side in a late-model Ford, and a gospel singer who was in charge of the music for the revival also drove by on the other side—singing as he went the chorus he was going to teach the children's choir that night: "Brighten the Corner Where You Are!" It was a poor black man who stopped to help. He put the badly beaten traveler in his rickety old car and drove him to the hospital in Albany, passing right by the church revival, where they were whooping it up on "Love Lifted Me." He left the man at the hospital and told the attendant he would stop back on Saturday to see about his patient and to pay any additional amount due.

Clarence's retelling of Jesus' parables occasioned all sorts of reactions.

One day a woman from Ellaville called about his "cotton patching" of the story of the Good Samaritan. Clarence had made a record of this particular parable, and apparently one of them had been circulated in Ellaville.

"I want to speak to Clarence Jordan."

"Yes. I am Clarence Jordan."

"Are you the preacher who did a record about a man that got beat up in Ellaville?"

"Yes, I did a record like that."

"Well, I live in Ellaville, and I want to know where that happened!"

Clarence tried to explain that the record was not the telling of an actual event; it was a contemporary version of the parable, designed to get the message of Jesus across in a South Georgia setting.

"Don't give me your theology," the woman insisted. "I want to know the truth. Where did this incident occur? Who was that man who got beat up? Who was that preacher, and who was the song leader who drove by? And who was that nigger that picked him up?"

"Ma'am, like I was saying, the story is not of an actual event. It—."

"Are you telling me it's a lie? It didn't happen? You made it up? And you call yourself a preacher? You are a liar, and worse, you make records of your lies and sell them! That's what I thought. You ought to be ashamed of yourself! Goodbye!"

BLAM!

Clarence pointed out that this incident was symbolic of the lives of many Christians. They love Jesus and know all the Bible stories by heart. They admire the Good Samaritan, living 2,000 years ago and doing his kind deed on a lonely road between Jerusalem and Jericho. But don't go and mess it up with modern relevance. That's a nice story about Jesus turning over the tables of the money changers in the temple in Jerusalem, but don't turn over any of the tables of *our* money changers in our temple! That was a great Sermon on the Mount that Jesus preached so long ago, but let's keep those enemies we're supposed to love in the distant past. Today we've got some real, live, ornery, *mean* enemies that Jesus didn't know about. We'll talk about loving enemies in the Sunday school class, but on Monday we've got to make bayonets, grenades, missiles, and nuclear bombs for our enemies. We'll love them after they're safely dead.

Jesus also said that unless a person gives up everything, he cannot be Jesus' disciple. Of course, that applied to the simple fishermen of His day who didn't have much to give up. Surely Jesus doesn't expect us to take Him literally and give up our cars and our air conditioners and our second homes and our fancy clothes and our investment portfolios? No, He doesn't mean that!

Then Clarence would thunder, "Yes, He *did* mean it! The gospel of Christ is eternally relevant. He still calls on us, today, to take up the cross and follow Him, down *our* roads, in South Georgia or wherever we live. He calls us to listen, and to obey!"

It was a powerful, exhilarating experience to be with Clarence and to realize the utter devotion he had to Christ. As time passed, I knew absolutely that God had led me there to be taught, to be strengthened, and to be prepared for exciting, sometimes trying, days ahead.

During that month at Koinonia, I transacted by phone most of the business necessary to liquidate my interest in the company. My partner and I had an agreement that if either of us wanted to leave the company, the other would have first option to buy the departing partner's share. He drove over to Koinonia one day and we discussed the sale, eventually working out the final details over the phone. In January I returned to Montgomery and signed a huge stack of legal papers, putting everything in his name. It would take a few years for all his payments to be made and all the money to be distributed to various Christian agencies and missions, but we were well on the way to becoming unburdened of our material things. We felt ready for whatever God had for us to do.

6
A New Kind of Partnership

When you ask the Lord for a job to do for Him, you can count on finding employment.

Two months after our stay at Koinonia, in the spring of 1966, I was back in New York City at the Broadway United Church of Christ, pastored by Dr. Lawrence Durgin. This time I was working out of an office in that building, contacting individuals and foundations to raise funds for Tougaloo College in Mississippi. During the counseling sessions that Linda and I had had with Dr. Durgin, he had suggested this position to me. Tougaloo, a small, predominantly black school related to the United Church of Christ and the Christian Church (Disciples of Christ), was launching a $10-million fund drive for new buildings and faculty salaries. Dr. Durgin, a trustee of the college, had persuaded me that my expertise in acquiring money could be better utilized in this new capacity.

I worked for Tougaloo for the next two years, organizing a development office in New York and traveling around the country and speaking on behalf of the college. During the summer of 1966, I took a leave of two months, however, and

Linda and I made the trip to Africa which I had turned down two years before. We visited church-sponsored schools, hospitals, refugee programs, agricultural projects. After that, my travel schedule included a lot more speaking at conferences and churches as I tried to interpret to Christians in America the tremendous needs I had observed in countries like Ghana, Tanzania, and Zaire.

During that time, the drastic reduction in our personal income necessitated a search for inexpensive living quarters. At one point during my Tougaloo job, our family (now five—Linda Faith was born in 1967) was living in a dingy apartment over a gas station in Glen Ridge, New Jersey, about forty minutes from New York City. In a wealthy commuting suburb of impressive homes, this particular building stuck out as something of an eyesore—which was, no doubt, why the rent was affordable.

About two blocks away stood a large, prestigious church, and the pastor, a friend of ours, asked me to preach there one Sunday. A few days before our agreed-upon date, he stopped in to see me.

"Millard," he announced with a chuckle, "I just thought you ought to know that I've had a couple of calls from parishioners this week. They've learned that you live in this scruffy apartment, and they aren't sure that you are a suitable person to speak in *our church!*"

I went anyway.

In May of 1968, the Tougaloo drive was well under way, with funds flowing in steadily for the buildings and salaries, and I was again looking for a specific personal challenge. The spirit and the fellowship which Linda and I had been a part of during our month at Koinonia two years earlier remained constantly on my mind. I felt pulled toward some kind of radical, dynamic Christian action, but I was unable to define what it might be.

I decided to resign my fund-raising position. Then I wrote to Clarence Jordan. I told him I was seeking to discover God's next job for me, and I asked what Clarence might have up his sleeve.

When he received my letter, Clarence phoned me immediately.

"Millard," he suggested, "maybe God has something up His sleeve for both of us. Let's get together and discuss it and pray about it."

The next weekend, Clarence was to preach a series of sermons in a Baptist church in Atlanta. I flew down there, and the pastor cheerfully turned over his study to us. For three days, whenever Clarence was not preaching in a service, we talked virtually nonstop.

Clarence was full of ideas about "partnership." He yearned to be God's partner, to be His person in the world, and to act from His perspective. As we shared and prayed together, I felt a growing excitement about the concept of reordering our lives in partnership with God and with one another.

During one of our discussions, the pastor of the church tapped lightly on the door.

"Excuse me for interrupting you," he said, "but I'm wondering if you would be willing to help me with a small practical problem we have here in the church. I need some advice and direction on this matter."

"Of course. Come in and sit down."

"I'll get right to the point," he said, pulling up a chair, "because I know your time is limited and you have much to talk about. Here's the situation. Our church janitor is a good one. We require him to work seven days a week; but we pay him only $80 a week. When I came to the church, his salary was only $50, but I made such a fuss that the deacons raised it to $80. That, however, is still not a decent wage. He lives all the way across town and has to drive about twenty miles round trip each day, just getting to and from work. We pay no transportation allowance. He has a wife and eight children to support. How can he live on $80 a week? I have pleaded with the deacons to raise his salary to a reasonable level, but they say we can't afford to; there's not enough money in the budget. What can I do? This thing is really bothering me."

He clasped his hands together, leaned forward, and rested

his arms on his knees. He looked first at me and then at Clarence. He repeated his question: "What can I do?"

Clarence was the first to speak, after several moments of penetrating silence. "John," he intoned, "you say the deacons refuse to raise his salary because there's no money. Is that right?"

"That's right, Clarence. They are just adamant about not adding more expense to our budget."

Clarence looked John squarely in the face. "John," he said, slowly, "maybe you don't need any more money. Let me ask you a few questions. First, where do you live?"

"Just down the street."

"How many children do you have?"

"Two."

"Do you make more than the janitor?"

John began to squirm. "Why, yes, Clarence. Yes, I do."

"Well, why not just swap salaries with him? That wouldn't require any extra money in your budget. You live right here by the church, so you don't have any commuting expenses, and you only have two children while he has eight. Surely you could live more easily on his salary than he can."

John, a white man, turned whiter. He hadn't expected that kind of solution.

Clarence was aware of his discomfort. "What's wrong, John? What's wrong with that solution? Is it contrary to Christian doctrine?"

"There's nothing at all wrong with it, Clarence, from a Christian point of view. That's why it upsets me!"

Clarence had seen the problem from God's perspective, and God loves janitors as much as He loves preachers! What a powerful insight. I thought to myself, *This* is what Jesus meant when He said to love our neighbors as we love ourselves. And that unless we give up everything we have, we cannot be His disciples. I wondered how John would handle the problem of the janitor's salary. I never found out. But I have the feeling that Clarence's words had a terrific impact on him—as they did on many people.

After John left, Clarence and I talked on and on about this

matter of seeing situations as God sees them. "God calls us," he said, "to be His prophetic people in practical, everyday situations, to be bold and radical in applying the way of Christ to all of our living."

Before the weekend ended, we had decided that the Fuller family should move to Koinonia to pursue further this exciting idea of partnership with God.

In 1968, Koinonia Farm was at a low point in its twenty-six-year history. The harassment, physical abuse, and economic boycott to which Koinonia's residents had been subjected over the years had taken a severe toll. From a high of about sixty residents during the 1950s, the population had dwindled until only two families remained: Florence and Clarence Jordan and their youngest son Lennie, and Will and Margaret Wittkamper and their youngest son Danny. Everybody else had left. As we talked that weekend in Atlanta, we thought that perhaps Koinonia Farm should be closed and a new center opened nearer to Atlanta. But for the moment we decided our family should move to the farm as soon as possible and make further decisions from there. A few weeks later we pulled into the driveway at Koinonia, wondering what kind of new ministry God had in store for us in Americus, Georgia.

During that summer, Clarence and I called together at Koinonia a small band of friends from around the country in whom we had great trust and confidence. We wanted to get their reactions and advice on everything we had talked and dreamed about. They included:

Bob Miller, alumni secretary for Union Theological Seminary and mayor of Englewood, New Jersey.

Ned Coll, a Catholic layman from Hartford, Connecticut, who founded the Revitalization Corps.

Ted Braun, of the Department of Interpretation of the United Church Board for World Ministries, New York City.

Bob Wood, a salesman for the Waterbury Tag Company in Westport, Connecticut.

Richard Jones, a black Baptist pastor from Brooklyn who

had recently become chaplain of Tougaloo College.

Leroy Ellis, a black businessman from Westport, Connecticut.

John Miller, from the Reba Place Fellowship in Evanston, Illinois.

Bob Swann, an active member of the Committee for Nonviolent Action, from Connecticut.

Sam Emerick, director of the Yokefellow Institute at Earlham College in Richmond, Indiana.

Ladon Sheats, a young IBM executive from New York.

Doc Champion, a local black Baptist pastor.

Slater King, a black businessman from Albany, Georgia.

The result of that meeting was a firm decision that we should remain at Koinonia and launch this concept of partnership with God and partnership with one another from that base. Using every available medium, we would begin to preach and teach about partnership; we would also put it into practice in three specific areas, which we would call "Partnership Farming," "Partnership Industries," and "Partnership Housing."

At that time no crops were being raised at Koinonia; the land was rented out for pasture, and the only "industry" was the mail order marketing of pecans and fruitcakes. We had few people and no money. But a large dream was gradually taking shape in all our minds, and we determined to move ahead on faith.*

We decided that a "fund for humanity" would be formed within the framework of Koinonia Partners (the name chosen for the new ministry), and money would be secured for it from two sources. First, we would begin Partnership Farming and Partnership Industries to feed money into the Fund for Humanity; second, concerned people throughout the country would be invited to make either gifts or noninterest loans. These funds would be earmarked for the "outreach" work of Koinonia Partners, mostly in constructing decent houses for low-income people in the area who were living in miserable shacks.

---

* The full story of the events at Koinonia, following that meeting, may be found in *The Cotton Patch Evidence* by Dallas Lee, New York, Harper & Row, 1971.

The new houses would be built on lots to be laid out on the north side of Koinonia Farm. They would have a cement floor, concrete block walls, and an asphalt shingle roof. They would be simple but adequate, complete with heating system, plumbing, electricity, and modern kitchen.

The unique feature of Partnership Housing was the financing system. We would obey the command of Exodus 22:25: "If you lend money to any of my people who are poor, do not act like a moneylender and require him to pay interest." We would build houses and add *no profit* to the cost of building and charge *no interest.* The people would be given twenty years to pay for their homes, and without interest the payments would be low enough for poor families to afford them. We wanted the houses to be a joy to people and not a burden.

As monthly payments began to come in, the money would go back into the Fund for Humanity to build more houses. We were well aware of the ravages of inflation on an investment that paid no return in the form of interest, but we were sure that three other factors in Partnership Housing would more than compensate for the lack of interest income. First, there would be a continuing appeal to people of financial means to share with the Fund for Humanity either through gifts or noninterest loans as an expression of their own discipleship. Second, there would be the steady flow of revenues from the other partnership enterprises. Finally, we would constantly challenge the families not only to make their monthly payments regularly but also to accelerate them if possible, and even to make extra contributions to the Fund for Humanity, as they could afford to do so, to help others who also wanted to get out of their rickety shacks. We envisioned a regenerative, ever-expanding Fund for Humanity, which would grow and blossom in the years ahead, building more and more houses for the poor at Koinonia, and expanding outward from there into Americus and beyond.

When we began laying out the first lots in late 1968, there wasn't enough cash on hand to build one house, but we were confident that the money would come. It did. The response to an October 1968 letter from Clarence to friends of Koinonia produced thousands of dollars. Forty-two lots and a community park were laid out and surveyed. The first two houses were soon under construction, in an area we called Koinonia Village.

Even though many people throughout the United States understood and supported this effort to relate the Gospel to the poor in tangible ways, many people did not, especially some of our closer neighbors.

As the first two houses were nearing completion, we called the local power company to request that they hook up the electricity. When their work crew arrived, I was at the building site. As the men began their job, the foreman of the crew sidled up to me and queried, "Who's building all these houses?" He swept his arm out, indicating the forty-two lots we had staked off.

"Koinonia is building them," I replied. "You know of Koinonia, don't you? We are a Christian community right down the road."

"Yes," he said, "I've heard of Koinonia. But why are you building all these houses?"

"We are building them for poor people—folks who don't have a decent house to live in. You've seen people around here living in bad houses, haven't you?"

"You mean those nigger shacks up and down the road?"

"Well, I wouldn't put it just like that, but you've got the idea."

"Okay, but I still don't understand. Who is making the money out of this project?"

"No one," I responded. "It is a Christian venture, and building these houses is an expression of our faith. The houses are sold to the people with no profit added to the cost of construction and no interest charged. The people will pay low monthly payments over a twenty-year period. We get the money for construction from gifts and noninterest loans from friends of Koinonia around the country and from shared profits of the Koinonia farming operations and the pecan-fruitcake-candy business."

"But why are you building the houses if no one is making any money out of it?"

I was becoming exasperated. "I've already told you," I said. "We are building them to help our neighbors who desperately need a decent house; we are doing this project because we are Christians and we believe Christians ought to help their neighbors when they are in need."

He shook his head in disbelief. "That's the craziest thing I've ever heard of!"

Now it was my turn to ask a question. "Sir," I said, "you've been grilling me about this project. Now I'd like to ask you a question. Are you by any chance a Christian?"

He drew himself up to his full stature and beamed with pride.

"Yes, sir, I'm a deacon in my church!"

"You're a deacon, and helping somebody is the craziest thing you've ever heard of?"

"Yes," he replied. "I've never heard of anything like this!" And he walked away, shaking his head.

Other local white people not only misunderstood the project but actively opposed it. When a local landowner learned that one of his "nigger families" was getting a new house at Koinonia, he ordered them to move off his land immediately. They had nowhere to go, because their house was not yet finished. So Koinonia let them move into one of the community guest houses while construction on their house was rushed to completion.

Another nearby farmer, learning that a family on his land was getting a new house at Koinonia, drove out to their shack with his shotgun and killed every one of their dogs.

One day a local farmer rode his big saddle horse into the new housing area and inquired where a particular family lived. I told him. Then he angrily informed me that a son of that man owed him some money. Snatching the horse's head around, he kicked him hard in the side, adding an oath, and headed for the man's house. When he got there, he steered the horse right up through a freshly planted lawn to the front door. He yelled out the alleged debtor's name. In a few moments, the father of the family came to the door. The man on the horse demanded to know where the son was.

"He owes me money!" he yelled.

The father said the boy wasn't at home.

"Tell that nigger he better get over to my house and pay me or I'll have his hide!"

With that stern warning, he jerked the horse's head and made him go in circles around and around the yard, tearing up all the newly planted grass with his hooves. When the man figured he'd done all the damage he could, he slapped his reins hard against the horse's neck, kicked him in the side, and galloped off.

I was furious at this contemptuous conduct, but the whole episode happened so quickly I really couldn't do anything. The old father was shaking with fright when I got to him. "Do you want me to try to do something about this?" I asked, pointing to the destroyed lawn.

"No sir. Forget it. He's upset 'cause we got such a nice place. My boy don't owe him no money. He's jus' mad 'bout us gettin' dis house. I don't think he'll be back."

And the man didn't come back. In time the local feelings of resentment among the whites subsided, and some people even began actively to encourage and support the work.

As for the black families who received the houses, they were absolutely ecstatic.*

Soon after moving into his new house, one man told me, "It's so good to live here. When it rains, I love to sit by the window and see it raining outside, and everything's all wet, and I'm sitting in here, and *it ain't raining on me!*"

One of the early families to move into Koinonia Village was Rose Belle and Willie James Reynolds and their children. They had been living on a country road south of Plains, in a terrible shack that leaked in every storm and was impossible to keep warm in winter. Willie and Rose Belle were so anxious to get out of that shack that they were in the new house the very day it was completed. The next evening, I walked up to Koinonia Village to see if they were getting settled with no

* The building program was not designed for blacks only. However, most of the really low-income people in that area were black, and the few whites who would have qualified for houses were not willing to live at Koinonia, either because of their own prejudice or out of fear of retaliation from other whites.

problems. Rose Belle was standing in the middle of the living room floor when I arrived. She grinned happily when she saw me.

"Come in! Come in!" she exclaimed.

"Rose Belle, I just stopped by to see if y'all are getting settled in okay."

"Millard, we are just fine. Everything is just fine."

"Well, good, but have you discovered any problems—anything that isn't satisfactory?"

"Oh, no. This house ain't *got* no problems! We are so happy to be in it. I tell you, Millard, being in this house is like we was dead and buried, and got dug up!"

Many times since that moment of exploding enthusiasm and gratitude in Rose Belle Reynolds's living room, I have pondered the powerful theological significance of her utterance, "dead, buried, and dug up." Rose Belle had never been to seminary, or college, or even high school. I know that she did not intend to make a profound statement, or that, even now, she feels that she said anything extraordinary. But surely this spontaneous exclamation of what she felt in her heart is a powerful symbolic expression of what the resurrected Christ is all about.

Rose Belle's heart was full, and her joy spilled over into mine. She had made it absolutely clear in her own earthy and inimitable way that love, to be real, must be put into action. And that we Christians had better be getting out our shovels and digging, for we are called to bring light to places where there is darkness, and to bring the resurrection of Christ to that which is "dead and buried." When this takes place, it strikes joy in the hearts of everyone involved—the ones doing the "digging," and the ones being "dug up"!

Ethel Dunning, a resident of Forest Park, the second housing community built at Koinonia, shared with me one day a powerful story illustrating this dimension of being "dug up."

Tom Dunning, his wife Ethel, and their children had been living in a shack on a nearby farm owned by a white lady. They came to Koinonia and were able to arrange to have a home built in Forest Park. Several weeks later, when their new house was just getting under construction, the white lady phoned Ethel and Tom to ask if what she had heard was true—namely, that they were having a new home built at Koinonia and that they would be leaving the farm when it was finished.

"Yes, ma'am, it's true," Ethel answered.

"Well," the lady replied, "I want to talk to you about this. Come to my house in the morning so we can discuss the matter."

Ethel went. She said the lady harangued her until midafternoon, shaming her for wanting to move to Koinonia. Ethel finally left in tears.

When she got back home, her water had been cut off. Both houses—Ethel and Tom's house and the lady's house—were served by a single well, with pipes running to both of them from a single pump. Of course, the lady owned the well, the pump, the pipes, and both houses; she had the legal right to cut off the water. And she used it.

For two months the Dunning family had to haul water in Tom's truck, filling buckets at a neighbor's house. One day, toward the end of this time, the lady phoned Ethel. She had a little problem.

"Ethel," she said, "my boy and his wife are coming to see us this weekend. Would you mind cooking us some of those special cakes you bake so well?"

"Yes, ma'am, I'd be glad to cook 'em—but you know I ain't got no water!"

"Oh, Ethel, that's right. I'd forgotten. Well, could you come over here to my house and bake them?"

At this point in her story, Ethel paused and looked straight at me for a long moment.

"Millard, you know what I did?"

"What?" I queried.

"I went over there and worked all day long baking those fancy cakes. I didn't say nothin' 'bout nothin'. I just baked and baked, and I was as nice as I could be. But you know what?"

"What, Ethel?"

"To do that, you'se got to be *dug up!*"

The message was clear. To be God's person, we must be "dug up," transformed, born again, given a new value system—one that enables us to bear insults and hurts, returning love for hate and good for evil. Ethel was able to do this. Sometime later, after Ethel and Tom had moved to their new house, the attitude of the white lady began to soften, and she has since visited in their home, expressing pleasure and happiness for them.

For four and a half years, until January 1973, Linda and I worked together in the blossoming ministry of Koinonia Partners. Linda, who had started off by typing correspondence and Clarence's translations, and processing pecan and cookbook orders, soon branched out to help organize a handcraft shop and a sewing industry. Later, a need arose for some kind of educational day-care facility for the preschool children who were moving into the new houses, and Linda launched the Koinonia Child Development Center. I was involved with the administrative end: overseeing the farming and partnership industries, supervising volunteers and work camps, writing publicity, and sharing the philosophy of this venture through speaking engagements.

Throughout this period, however, my real concern was the continuing expansion of the home-building program. And as the houses went up, our goal was always to put love in the mortar joints—to be God's "dug up" workers, using His shovels to help His people in need.

7
To Mbandaka and Back

By 1972, Koinonia Village was virtually complete; twenty-seven families were living in their new homes on 100-by-200-foot lots. Several lots had been reserved for recreation areas, and two more were used for the child development center and a nursery for preschoolers.

Early that same year, we had laid out plans for Forest Park, another housing site for thirty-two homes on three-quarter-acre lots about a mile down the road from Koinonia Village. Don Mosley, a talented engineer from Waco, Texas, had first come to Koinonia in 1970 as a volunteer. Now Don and Carolyn and their two children had become "resident partners"—members of the community on a long-term basis. Don had planned and installed the water system at Koinonia Village. Then he designed a unique layout for the new Forest Park development. In this community the houses are all oriented toward each other across a series of small parks; the backs of the houses, with utility areas and gardens, are toward the road.

Both the resident community and the ministry of Koinonia Partners had been growing steadily. Clarence Jordan's sudden death in 1969, as he sat in his little writing shack working on one of his powerful sermons, had left a great emptiness within those of us who knew and loved him. At the same time, the strength of his leadership continued to motivate us all. New and very able people were arriving at Koinonia, many deeply committed to the partnership housing program. I knew the project would continue to expand without my being on the scene.

Linda and I began to wonder whether another housing project, financed by the same principles as Koinonia's Fund for Humanity, could be launched in Zaire. When we had visited the country briefly on our mission tour six years earlier, we had seen a struggling cement-block-making plant along the Zaire (formerly Congo) River in the city of Mbandaka, about 400 miles upriver from the capital city of Kinshasa. The church had purchased this enterprise from a Belgian businessman who fled at the time Zaire received independence in 1960. An effort was being made to alleviate the area's desperately high unemployment through the production of sand and cement blocks, as well as through several other small church-sponsored economic development projects.

The needs were indeed overwhelming. Linda and I had never been able to stop thinking about the miserable shantytowns we had passed in Mbandaka. The city had grown from a populace of 30,000 to 150,000 in the thirteen years since independence, as droves of people, formerly restricted by law to their jungle villages, now flocked to the city in a vain search for the Promised Land.

When they arrived, there was no place for them to live. The cardboard and mud and thatch huts that they threw up wherever they found space were hopelessly inadequate in the recurring tropical storms; and with an unemployment rate running close to 50 percent, there were few people who succeeded in finding jobs to improve their dismal situation.

Could we possibly make any dent at all in this enormous pile of problems? We couldn't—but we knew God could. And we felt sure that He was urging us to go.

We began by contacting Dr. Robert G. Nelson, Africa Secretary for the Christian Church (Disciples of Christ). Bob had made all the arrangements for our short visit to Zaire in 1966, and we asked him about the possibilities of a longer term of service there.

"Millard," he exulted over the telephone, "only yesterday a representative of the Zaire church was in my office asking for someone to help them with development. I told them we didn't have anyone—but now I can tell them we do!"

From there on, things kept falling into place so neatly that we knew our destination was the right one. So we packed up our family—four children now, including eighteen-month-old Georgia—and after six months of study and orientation, three of them in Paris learning French, we headed for Africa. We arrived in Mbandaka, Zaire, in July of 1973.

We first set about to revitalize the collection of ancient, dilapidated equipment and the discouraged, often unpaid, workers at the block and sand project. We started a Mbandaka Fund for Humanity, and Koinonia Partners sent the initial gift in the amount of $3,000. Then we plunged in to inaugurate the building of houses. They were simple, solid cement-block structures without available electricity or running water, but they seemed truly heaven-sent to families whose mud-brick, dirt-floored huts were literally crumbling around them.

Mbokolo, the father of one of the families who moved to the new project, and an enthusiastic Christian who became my great friend during our stay in Zaire, expressed precisely this sentiment to me.

"On the day we learned we had been chosen to have a new house," he said, "we were so full of joy, to receive this gold from heaven! The announcement of this good news was, for me, like the announcement of the birth of a new baby in my house, and even greater than that. Why? Because I have children, given to me by God, but I never had enough money to build them a decent house. Thanks to my brothers and sisters in Christ, I live today in *une belle maison* [a beautiful house]!"

And Nkota, a young mother, called her new house "a gift which fell to me from heaven. It demonstrates the power of God," she told us, "who acts through those who listen to Him, to spread the Good News."

Throughout our three years in Zaire, however, we had to struggle against frustration and discouragement. We agonized over widespread ignorance, thievery, and disease. As the new white folks in town, we were constantly being arrested on nonsensical charges. We encountered obstructionist bureaucrats and official red tape more incredibly mind-boggling than anything ever thought of by the United States.

But this was God's project, and He kept upholding us. Eventually we were able to persuade the local government to *give* the church enough land for 114 houses right in the center of the city, and within a year we had received nearly 5,000 written applications for those houses.

When we learned that this piece of ground was called Bokotola by the local people, we realized once again that the Lord always knows what He's doing. The reason this land stood empty was that during colonial days it had served as a permanent buffer strip between the white Europeans' homes and those of the blacks.

The Belgians euphemistically called the land the "health strip," but the Zairois more accurately referred to it as Bokotola, which means "man who does not care for others." Now, in the name of Christ, new homes for the poorest of His people were covering this old territory, which formerly represented prejudice and alienation. Furthermore, both our financial support and the volunteers from the United States and Canada who began arriving to help us came from a wide variety of Christian groups—Baptist, Methodist, Presbyterian, Lutheran, United Church of Christ, Disciples, Mennonite, Episcopalian, Roman Catholic, Quaker, Reformed Church in America, Hutterite—another beautiful witness to the unity we have in His service. On July 4, 1976, at the dedication service for the new community, its name was officially changed. It is now called Losanganya, which means "reconciler, reunifier, everyone together."

By the time our family left Zaire in 1976, all the 114 houses originally planned in Mbandaka were begun. Many were completed, with hundreds of people already living in the development, and the government had given us an adjoining parcel of land on which we had laid out lots for 56 more houses. In addition, the new project in the village of Ntondo was getting under way.

We were able to leave the projects at that stage because they were in the hands of outstanding leadership, both African and American. I knew that if they were to continue to expand—and many other towns were clamoring for their own building programs—we would have to raise more funds. Great numbers of people needed to be persuaded to become partners in this ministry.

We hoped to convince friends at home to share their money as well as their talents, to make possible the construction of many more houses. We also needed funds to be able to continue providing artificial limbs for those who needed them. This effort had begun after we encountered dozens of people in Zaire who had become helpless beggars following an accident or infection which caused them to lose a leg. For about $200, a person could be fitted with a new limb, in the process acquiring dignity and pride, as well as employability. By 1980, sixty men and women had received artificial legs through this Rise Up and Walk program.

At the very least, we hoped to persuade Americans to send us their old eyeglasses. There was absolutely no source of glasses in the Mbandaka area, and when churches at home began shipping us barrels of secondhand ones, we sold them at $2 a pair. By the time 1,000 people had received otherwise unobtainable eyeglasses, we had acquired enough cash to build another house!

So there were plenty of needs and possibilities and opportunities to ponder during our long trip home.

We arrived back at Koinonia in August of 1976. The Forest Park development was almost complete, and it was exciting to see all the new houses that had gone up there in our absence. But some big questions kept going around in my mind. "Lord, just where do we go from here? What are You calling us to do now with this new concept of mission?"

Eight years earlier, when Clarence Jordan and I were struggling to chart a fresh course for Koinonia, we had called together a group of deeply committed Christian friends for advice and assistance. So in September of 1976 I put out a call again, and this time twenty-seven people responded. They traveled to Koinonia from nine states, at their own expense, and some also helped with ticket money so that Sam Mompongo could come from the project just beginning in Ntondo, Zaire.

For three days we prayed and dreamed and discussed and brainstormed together. Out of this conference came the decision to form a new organization which would work in community building wherever the Lord might lead. We chose the name Habitat for Humanity. Initially we would be headquartered at Koinonia, and we would seek always to have a close working relationship with Koinonia Partners, but eventually we would look for a separate location nearby, probably in the town of Americus.

We also made plans that weekend to hold a formal organization meeting the following March at Stony Point, New York. There we would develop a constitution and bylaws and elect our first directors.

There was unanimous agreement that Habitat for Humanity would always be thoroughly ecumenical; that it would remain a low-overhead operation, financed in each location by a revolving Fund for Humanity; that it would serve as a facilitating group, linking resources with people in need through existing structures. As a perfect example of this kind of cooperation, we met that weekend with Ryan and Karen Karis, who were then living at Koinonia, and who had volunteered to go to Ntondo to do the surveying for the new project. In November 1976, the Christian Church (Disciples of Christ) agreed to support Ryan, a Quaker, and Karen, a Lutheran, for two months, to work under Habitat for Humanity with the Baptist community sponsoring the project in Ntondo!

A vital role to be filled by Koinonia Partners would be the training of builders and community development workers. Volunteers could come and work in the already established housing program at Koinonia, making a real contribution there even as they were receiving training for some other project—all at little or no cost to Habitat.

As short-range plans were being laid, we also did a lot of dreaming about longer-range possibilities. Not too many years earlier I had set myself a goal: to become a millionaire as quickly as possible. Now my life had new goals. Could we be so bold as to think of building *enough houses for a million people?*

Why not? Why not even more?

When we began the first house at Koinonia, and again when we began the first house in Mbandaka, and in Ntondo—we didn't have enough money for any of them. But ours was a ministry of faith, and as long as we relied on God for our resources, He would surely continue to supply all our needs. As the twenty-seven of us dispersed at the end of our brainstorming weekend, we knew that God had truly been at work among us, and we looked forward with joy to the unfolding of the plans He had set in motion.

8
The Economics of Jesus

Back in the summer of 1969, I was invited to speak at a United Church of Christ conference in Indianapolis. One of the themes I used in my presentations there was Jesus' firm command to lay up your treasures not on earth, but in heaven.

After one of these sessions, Fred Dare, an insurance salesman from Muncie, Indiana, came up to introduce himself. It had been bothering him, he said, that every working day of his life was spent persuading people to "lay up treasures on earth," and that, in fact, he was seeking to do the same thing himself.

A few weeks later Fred made a trip to Koinonia. He spent a week there with us, thinking about his faith, praying, discussing, and sometimes just walking in the woods.

Finally he made a bold decision.

He would quit his job immediately, and he would make himself available for God's service on a full-time basis. The one stumbling block to this course was that he had a wife and family to support, and he didn't have any significant savings.

He quit his job anyway.

In the next few weeks he began to spend all his time in the heart of Muncie, doing what he could for the poor of that city. He worked without pay. All the time he kept praying that God would open the right door, one that would offer some opportunity as a full-time Christian worker, with enough income to support his family.

Months went by. No regular job. No steady income. Fred had to borrow money for groceries and other necessities. But he never wavered in his faith that God had called him to make the break from his secular employment and that, in time, he would find the job God had for him.

At first Fred wrote to me regularly, but as his waiting continued I didn't hear as often. Then one morning, almost a year later, I received an excited letter from him.

> Millard, I've been offered a job as lay pastor on an Indian reservation in Mandaree, North Dakota, by the United Church Board for Homeland Ministries. I believe this is what I've been waiting for. And Nancy is positive about it, too. There's only one problem. As you know, I'm in debt, and now it's up to five thousand dollars. I can't just walk off and leave my creditors holding the bag; neither can I send them the money from North Dakota, because my salary will be too small to make the payments, let alone the rapidly accumulating interest charges. I hesitate to write you about this need, but somehow I feel that the Lord may be able to help me through you.

"How?"I wondered aloud, as I finished reading. The Fund for Humanity was broke, as usual, and urgently needed funds to continue building houses for the poor at Koinonia.

Later, as I walked from the office to the community dining room for lunch, a distance of about a hundred yards, I was still wondering how I could possibly help Fred.

After the noon meal, I was ambling back to my office and still pondering this need, when Peter Clarke strode up beside me. Peter was a young student volunteer from Rochester, New York, who had been working at the farm all summer.

"Could I talk to you sometime?"

"Sure, Peter. What about right now?"

"That's fine."

"Come on over to the office."

Peter didn't even wait until we got to the office. He had something on his mind, and he was anxious to share it.

"Millard, I've been here all summer, and my faith has deepened considerably. This experience has meant a great deal to me. I only wish I could stay longer, but I have to leave tomorrow. Before I go, though, I want to ask you something."

By this time we were in my office, and both of us pulled up a chair and sat down.

"Since I was a boy, Millard, I've been saving money. Most of it I made as a paperboy. Now, after experiencing Koinonia, I feel a strong urge to make this money available for the Lord's work. I may need it later on if I decide to attend medical school, but in the meantime, do you have any ideas on how it could best be used?"

"Maybe I do, Peter. Let me tell you a story."

I leaned forward and told Peter all about Fred Dare. How I met him, his visit to Koinonia, his resignation from his job, and his months of volunteer effort without pay while he looked for full-time work in Christian service.

Then I reached over on my desk and picked up the letter from Fred that had arrived an hour earlier. I shoved it into Peter's hands.

"Read that," I said.

Peter focused his eyes on the unfamiliar handwriting of this total stranger. I watched him intently as he read. When he got to the place in Fred's letter that told how much money he needed, Peter looked up at me in astonishment and exclaimed, "This is incredible!"

"How's that, Peter?"

"This man needs exactly the amount of money I have in my savings account! When did you get this letter?"

"This morning. About an hour ago."

"Incredible. Incredible." He kept shaking his head as he resumed reading. When he finished the letter, he read it again. Then he looked up at me a second time.

"What do you think, Millard?"

"I think maybe the Lord answered your prayer real fast!"

"Yeah. For sure. I think you're right."

"Peter, let me make a suggestion. Go home. Think and pray some more about this. Then if you still feel led to meet this need, send me your check made out to the Fund for Humanity. We'll enter it in our books as a noninterest loan. Then we'll send the money immediately to Fred as a noninterest loan. He can pay off his debts, take the job in North Dakota, and pay the loan back to the fund as he can afford to. In that way, you'll have the money, the Fund for Humanity will have the money, Fred will have the money, Fred's creditors will have their money, the Indian church will have a pastor, and, most important of all, the Lord's work will be getting done! Of course, you'll have to trust Fred, a total stranger, for the repayment if you ever need it for medical school."

"Okay, Millard. But I think I already know my answer."

Peter left the next day. A week later, we received his check for $5,000. It was promptly sent to Fred with a letter explaining the miraculous way in which the money had been provided. You can imagine his rejoicing! Fred paid off his debts, took the job with the Homeland Board, and moved his family to Mandaree, North Dakota.

In the months that followed, Fred faithfully made payments on the loan. About a year later, I received a letter from Peter Clarke. He had finally made a decision to enter medical school, and he would need a specific sum of money for his initial fees. I went to the loan repayment card for Fred Dare and discovered that he had sent back *exactly* that amount!

In the ensuing years, Fred served faithfully in Mandaree, and Peter studied medicine. All the while, Fred regularly paid on his debt until it was completely liquidated. Even as he repaid Peter's loan, Fred contributed generously to the Koinonia Fund for Humanity, and after we moved to Zaire in 1973 and set up a Fund for Humanity there, he contributed to that as well.

Peter Clarke kept up his interest, too, and in the summer of 1974 he came to Zaire to visit us and to work for three months at the mission hospital in Ntondo.

In 1977, Fred Dare returned to Muncie to pastor a local

United Church of Christ, and he received full ordination a year later. Since then his congregation has raised many hundreds of dollars for the Habitat projects in Zaire, and in the summer of 1979 he brought a work camp of young people from his church to Americus to help with home-building there. As soon as he returned home, Fred started raising funds to help buy a much-needed pickup truck for the Habitat crew in Americus. That same year, Peter Clarke graduated from medical school in Belgium.

The story of Fred Dare and Peter Clarke is just one of dozens I can cite when folks inquire, as they so often do, "Exactly where does the money come from for all these houses?"

It comes from operating within God's perspective, which usually sees situations just about reversed from the way the world sees them. When we start looking at things the way God does, we discover that we have been plugged into some powerful Kingdom ideas, especially Kingdom economics.

I have long believed that every Christian seminary should offer a required first-year course titled "Economics of Jesus 101." The thrust of this study would be so radically different from other courses that it might well cause students to restructure their seminary programs completely—perhaps their entire lives. Certainly it could have a radical effect on the churches they would serve in years to come.

The textbook for this course would dwell at length on several vital Biblical principles. For example, *Jesus can multiply the minute to accomplish the gigantic.*

The most obvious documentation for this principle appears in the six different Gospel accounts of the feeding of the multitudes. Each time, the scriptures tell us, Jesus started with a few chunks of bread and fish.

I can imagine the disciples looking at that small handful of food and then casting their eyes across the vast throng of humanity before them.

"Not nearly enough."

"No way!"

"Pitiful."

"Impossible!"

I can hear them whispering among themselves. The disciples, looking through eyes of practicality mingled with their ever present doubts, see only the smallness of the resources and the enormity of the need.

Jesus, however, sees the situation entirely differently. He takes the small amount of bread and fish in His hands, and lifting His eyes heavenward, He begins to pray.

"Father, we thank You for this food. Thank You."

Then Jesus calmly turns to his disciples.

"Okay, now divide the people into groups of about fifty, and pass out the loaves and the fishes."

Can you imagine the incredulous looks on their faces when they hear this order?

"John, did you hear what Jesus said? *You* pass out the food!"

"No, Peter, how about *you* doing it?"

Jesus' steady gaze finally gets them going. They enter the crowd and haltingly, hesitantly, start giving each person some bread and fish. And as every Sunday school student knows, they not only have enough for everybody, but they also gather up basketfuls of leftovers.

The economic lessons we must learn from these great miracles of our Lord are, first, to take whatever is available in a given situation of need (all of it!); second, to thank God and ask for His blessing; third, to get ourselves organized; and finally, to launch an effort to meet the need with those available resources. When we move out in faith, God moves, too, and our small supplies are miraculously multiplied to fill the need.

One of the devil's neatest (and most successful) tricks is to convince us that a problem is too big—that it would be folly to tackle such a major need with such meager resources. "Better quit; give up; or better still, don't start!" the devil whispers in our attentive ears. And how often that tactic works, even though we Christians have at our disposal the effective, and proven, economics of Jesus, which expand the small, upon being blessed by God, into a gracious plenty.

When the first Fund for Humanity was set up at Koinonia

in 1968, we had so little—only the land and a dream, but no money. Nevertheless, we thanked God for what we had, got organized, and launched out in faith. The building program has never stopped. By 1980, nearly 100 homes had been built at Koinonia and in Americus, and new ones were going up at the rate of one every three to four weeks.

The manner in which these houses are financed illustrates another aspect of Kingdom economics. "If a fellow . . . living near you becomes poor . . . do not make him pay interest on the money you lend him, and do not make a profit on the food you sell him."[1] *In our dealings with poor people, we are to charge no interest and seek no profit.*

Now this sort of system is foolish in the eyes of the world. In fact, on the rare occasions when poor people I have known have been able to obtain any kind of loan at all, it was only through a finance company that charged a much higher rate of interest than standard lending institutions. As a banker friend of mine likes to say, "In order to be able to get a loan easily, you have to have a financial statement that shows you really don't need the money!"

Recently I came across these interesting lines from that compelling Christian thinker, C.S. Lewis:

> There is one bit of advice given to us by the ancient heathen Greeks, and by the Jews in the Old Testament, and by the great Christian teachers of the Middle Ages, which the modern economic system has completely disobeyed. All these people told us not to lend money at interest; and lending money at interest—what we call investment—is the basis of our whole system. . . . I am not an economist, and I simply do not know whether the investment system is responsible for the state we are in or not. This is where we want the Christian economist. But I should not have been honest if I had not told you that three great civilizations had agreed . . . in condemning the very thing on which we have based our whole life.[2]

The concept of no profit and no interest is absolutely essential in building homes for the poor. Interest is a burden that keeps poor people locked into their situation. It is a great barrier that they cannot climb over to escape their miserable life-style. But Jesus' followers don't have to make a profit—they are more interested in people than in profits. Why? Because they walk in His footsteps. How much did He charge for His healing services? Or for all that food He distributed? Or for His incomparable skills as a teacher? And what was His fee for raising Lazarus and others from the dead?

The economics of Jesus puts no value on profit or interest—but tremendous emphasis on meeting human need.

Whenever a house is built by Habitat, it is financed by a local Fund for Humanity, with no interest or profit, and usually twenty years to pay. Money to work with comes from house payments of completed units, from the shared revenues of enterprises at Koinonia and at other locations, and from gifts and noninterest loans sent by churches and individuals in many parts of the world.

How can such a system work, let alone expand? In an inflationary economy, not to charge interest makes no sense; the investment diminishes with every passing month. Still, the voice of Jesus keeps saying, "Feed my people."

"But how, Lord?"

He will show us how. As our circle of concern enlarges, and more and more people are moved to share, the damage done by inflation is repaired by new gifts, and the lack of interest income is compensated for by ever-widening participation. If our motivation is simply to help and to minister in Christ's name, the miracle can occur again.

In the summer of 1977 I was invited by Dr. Harry Bredeweg, conference minister, to speak at the annual meeting of the Indiana-Kentucky Conference of the United Church of Christ. A number of churches in that conference were already actively interested in the Habitat building program. At that gathering, a pledge was made by the 204 congregations of the conference to raise $100,000 during 1978, to build fifty houses in Ntondo.

The idea caught fire. In one association, each of twenty-two churches was given $25 as seed money and instructed to make it grow in the manner of the New Testament parable of the talents. Three months later, at their next meeting, these churches laid their "increase" on the altar. Twenty-two mostly small, rural congregations had raised more than $25,000! And the full 1978 goal of $100,000 had been reached *before the end of 1977!*

During the following year the conference decided to double its pledge, to $200,000—and that was met. In 1979, more funds came in, and at year's end more than $225,000 had been raised, enough to build 113 houses. At the same time, the giving of these churches to their other denominational obligations increased also. When the economics of Jesus begins to operate, there's always enough for the need—and enough for other needs as well!*

Not only did these folks organize cake sales and concerts and concessions at church softball games and implement all sorts of other ingenious fund-raising ideas, but they generated enthusiasm, which brought new workers. In fact, we have enjoyed the participation of a veritable parade of Habitat volunteers and work-camp groups from Indiana!

In Manitoba, Canada, a group of Hutterite colonies provided another impressive example of the economics of Jesus. During 1979 they contributed $6,000 to build homes in Zaire; then they proceeded to obtain, through the Mennonite Central Committee, a three-for-one matching grant from the Canadian International Development Agency—and their gift immediately became $24,000. The following year they gave $5,000, which was matched in the same fashion. A few hundred people in these Christian farming colonies had thereby generated a total of $44,000 for the work in Zaire.

The miracle will happen again and again, as it did when

---

* In a letter to a fellow clergyman on September 22, 1978, Dr. Bredeweg described the effect of the Habitat pledge on conference giving during the previous year: "Our total church giving went up nearly $170,000, of which the Zaire project is only $100,000; so it would be my judgment that the project inspired greater giving rather than hindering the giving of our people. It certainly has given our people a new spirit and a sense of joy that is unbelievable. I can recommend the project without any reservations whatsoever."

At the close of the following year, during which time the conference raised its second $100,000 for Habitat, Dr. Bredeweg was able to write in the conference newsletter: "I am proud to say that during this past year . . . we experienced the largest gain in basic support for our Christian World Mission in our conference's history!"

multitudes were fed in Galilee—but not if we insist on waiting until we think we have "enough." We must follow Jesus' instructions: Pass out what you've got. And have faith.

Which brings us to another important principle. *Jesus expects us to pass out* all *we've got, as He did with the loaves and the fishes.*

At Koinonia, as soon as we inauguarated the Fund for Humanity, it was always broke. Whatever money came in was immediately spent on building more houses. Nothing was held back for investments or endowments. If cash became available faster than we had anticipated, we simply built faster to use it up. We wanted only to invest in the people we sought to serve, and the endowment of the Fund for Humanity became an ever-enlarging number of houses.

The New Testament records that when the believers shared *all* their belongings, "there was no one in the group who was in need . . . and God poured rich blessings on them all."[3] But when Ananias and Sapphira tried to share *some* of their wealth and secretly to withhold the rest, the judgment upon them was swift and terrible.[4]

There is an important corollary to the last principle, and Christians who seek to follow the economics of Jesus have a real obligation to broadcast it to the whole world. *Without question, the poverty of the "have-nots" is directly related to the riches of the "haves."*

We live in an age when one family in the United States can casually spend on a single luxurious restaurant dinner as much money as another family in the Third World is able to earn in an entire year. Hunger and desperate need exist alongside enormous wealth in any country we might name; yet knowledgeable scientists repeatedly insist that the earth's resources, properly managed, could provide a decent living standard for every single human being.

God does not mean for His people to go hungry or to do without adequate clothing and shelter. And the answer of Kingdom economics to the terrible gap between poverty and affluence is clearly stated by John the Baptist: "Whoever has two shirts must give one to the man who has none, and whoever has food must share it."[5] This is outrageously simple. And it is the only solution that will work.

A few years ago I spoke at a meeting in a large church in Florida, using this text from Luke for my talk. I knew that many people in that church had a house in Florida and another one (or two) up North. So I decided to make the scripture as relevant as possible.

"I wonder if this teaching of John about shirts could also be applied to houses?" I asked.

I really didn't expect an answer, but I wanted to start people thinking—and maybe cause them to squirm a bit!

But one man did respond. He popped up, obviously stung by the question, and blurted out, "Mr. Fuller, excuse me. I don't think you really wanted an answer to that question, but I've got to say something. I think your analogy between shirts and houses is unfair. After all, a person can't really wear more than one shirt at a time, but he—uh—he—."

And the man sat down.

John's teaching certainly does have something to do with houses, and automobiles, and jewelry, and bank accounts, and all the rest of our possessions. There is a direct line connecting the two- and three-house person with the no-house person. And that early Baptist evangelist is calling us to see the connection.

Two people who have seen it are Bob and Myrna Gemmer, of St. Petersburg, Florida. They visited us in Zaire in 1975, and they have taken a tremendous interest in Habitat for Humanity; Bob has served on the Board of Directors ever since the group officially organized in 1977. In 1978 the Gemmers were instrumental in launching a new Habitat project for migrant workers in Immokalee, Florida. And they decided that by selling their lovely second home in Ohio and donating the proceeds to Habitat, they could provide funds to build houses for several families in Immokalee. When they did this, the Church of the Brethren agreed to match their Biblical gift—and once again the multiplying effect of the economics of Jesus produced substantial results!

Not all families have a second home to give away. But most

of the families I talk with in American churches do live in comfortable houses. Some of them, expressing tangibly their desire to share this blessing, have begun to tithe their rent or house payments to Habitat for Humanity.

My friend Ethel Dunning at Koinonia, who handled her relationship with her white landlady in such a beautifully Christian way, had some pungent remarks for me on the subject of sharing.

In the spring of 1978, I was invited to speak at a Southern Baptist Christian Life Seminar in Nashville, Tennessee, on the subject "Economics: Toward a Life-style for Christians." I decided to consult Ethel on what I should say.

The afternoon I went to see her, she was sitting on the front porch. I walked up and greeted her.

"Ethel, how you doing?"

"Oh, jes' fine," she replied. "How you gettin' along?"

We exchanged a few pleasantries, and then I asked, "Look, Ethel, I came over here because I've got a problem. I need your advice. I've been invited to speak to 600 or 700 Southern Baptists, a lot of them preachers, up in Nashville, Tennessee, and I want you to give me some ideas on what I should say to them. The topic they've asked me to talk on is economics—you know, about money and possessions and what kind of life-style Christians ought to be living in regard to these things."

She squinted and fixed me with a firm stare.

"Millard," and she slowly squeezed out her words, "that's a good subject!" She added, after a pause, "And that's a good congregation to hear it! Yes, sir!" She paused again.

"Millard, I tell you what you gotta do. You jes' go up there to Nashville and tell those Baptists there ain't *no* way you can live in big houses with lots of money and plenty of food and they is po' folks all around you livin' in shacks and hongry and God is gonna be happy with *you!*"

I told the people at the seminar exactly what Ethel had said. And it is only as all Christians attempt to get this message out to the world that we will even begin to deal with the needs around us. Jesus teaches us that it is more blessed to give; we are called to spread out that blessing!

Another aspect of Jesus' economics which the world has not accepted is that *each human life, no matter how insignificant it may seem, is priceless.*

Remember when Jesus encountered the man from Gadara who was possessed by demons?[6] He was so crazy, Mark tells us, that he lived in caves and raced around the countryside hollering and screaming, cutting himself with jagged stones, and refusing even to wear clothing. When Jesus healed the man, the evil spirits went into a herd of 2,000 hogs, which then rushed headlong into the sea and drowned. In the next scene we find the wild man sitting calmly with Jesus and His disciples, clothed and in his right mind.

What is the key to this weird tale? Clarence Jordan surmised that the man was probably a Jew from Palestine, possibly even the prodigal son in "the far country." Although he had been taught from his youth not to have anything to do with hogs, he had gone to this strange land, right on the eastern shore of the Sea of Galilee, and had become involved in a "bootleg" hog operation that was probably "ham-running" pork over to Palestine, a hog-dry state. Eventually his hog life-style, going counter to his religious beliefs, had driven him nuts.

Jesus knew that in order to save the man, He had to deal with the situation that had created the problem, namely, the hogs. So without hesitation He caused the destruction of all 2,000 in order to restore sanity and bring salvation to one insignificant crazy man.

For Jesus and His disciples, there was cause for great rejoicing: the sick person had been made whole. But from the hog owners there was only moaning and groaning. They had suffered a monetary loss. The wild man was miraculously healed, but at what price? He wasn't worth that much! And a great hue and cry was sent up for Jesus to leave the territory.

In many other scripture passages we see Jesus placing enormous value on people the world regards as unimportant. Consider His dealings with Zacchaeus, the despised tax collector,[7] or the prostitute who washes His feet with her hair,[8] or the related parables of the lost sheep, the lost coin, and the prodigal son.[9] Whenever the welfare of a human being hangs in the balance, *no* expenditure of time or effort or money is too high.

Perhaps the most difficult principle in Jesus' economics for the world to comprehend is illustrated in the parable of the laborers in the vineyard.[10] In that story all the workers, regardless of the time of day at which they started, are paid the same wage at the end of the day.

Why? Because in Kingdom economics, *the needs of people are paramount, and the response to those needs is not connected in any way with people's usefulness or productivity.* Grace and love abound for all. Equally.

Christians today like to talk about this kind of unmerited love, but when it comes to practical experience, their ire is often aroused. They like to spiritualize the message of the parable and to apply it only to those persons who are "saved" at the last moment before their death. Such an interpretation comfortably waters down this really powerful teaching of Jesus.

The early Christians, however, understood it, as well as the related messages of Jesus about undeserved love and mercy, in a much more inclusive and practical way. The believers all shared everything they had with one another, and sold their property and belongings, and divided the money with all the rest—on the basis of need.[11] And in Jesus' parable, the employer reminds the workers who are grumbling that he has paid every single person a fair day's wage. "Now take your pay and go home. . . . Don't I have a right to do as I wish with my own money? Or are you jealous because I am generous?"

Of course we are. Envious, confused, incredulous. Because we haven't yet learned to see with God's perspective. Instead, we are confined by our own selfish tunnel vision.

But when we step out in faith, following the new economics Jesus taught, our horizons suddenly expand fantastically. And when we trust Him completely, sharing and sacrificing without seeking profits, making need and not our narrow standard of merit the criterion, He will take our small gifts and multiply them to incredible dimensions.

The economics of Jesus forms the solid foundation on which Habitat for Humanity is building.

---

1. Leviticus 25:35, 37.
2. *The Joyful Christian, 127 Readings from C. S. Lewis,* New York, Macmillan, 1977, p. 185.
3. Acts 4:34a, 33b.
4. Acts 5:1-11.
5. Luke 3:11.
6. Mark 5:1-20.
7. Luke 19:1-10.
8. Luke 7:36-50.
9. Luke 15:1-32.
10. Matthew 20:1-16.
11. Acts 2:44-45.

9
A Step in Faith: San Antonio

A great source of strength for Linda and me while we were in Zaire was our correspondence with Christian friends back home. On the days when our creaky block-and-sand machinery broke down, or the weather looked threatening and half our work crew stayed home, or I went into town for the mail and ended up wasting half the day being arrested on some ludicrous charge—on these days, letters of support from people at home were more than welcome. We knew that there were lots of folks who cared about us and our work, but when they wrote long, newsy epistles and told us of their regular prayers on our behalf, that was even more encouraging. And when our construction funds were low, as they always were, and a letter arrived announcing that someone's church had just voted to raise enough money to build another house in Zaire—well, that was *really* cause for thanksgiving!

The faithful correspondence of Birdie Lytle, back in San Antonio, Texas, was the sort we loved to receive. Birdie and her husband Bill, a Presbyterian pastor, had visited us at Koinonia years before. They stayed there a couple of days, helping to pack pecans while one of their children baby-sat with our children, and a friendship developed between our families, which we have treasured ever since.

At the beginning of 1976, when our term in Zaire was drawing to a close, we received one letter from Birdie which was particularly notable. Optimistic and full of interesting conversation as always, it also contained an unexpected question.

> Millard, what do you think about the possibility of a Fund-for-Humanity-type project in the inner city? I've been working in San Antonio with a food pantry for the needy, and there is a center there where a young couple provide a wonderful, caring recreation program for teenagers. But the housing is awful, and the people who live in the area have absolutely no prospect of ever finding anything better. The problem is so huge I would scarcely know where to start, but it seems to me that if a few Christians were to get together with a lot of faith and determination, we could do *something!*

I could hardly wait to get a piece of airmail paper into the typewriter. Letters between Zaire and the United States often took many weeks. Sometimes they were opened and enclosures were stolen; sometimes they never arrived at all. I wanted to get a reply started on its way to Birdie immediately. After nearly five years of building at Koinonia, and three more in Zaire under totally different circumstances, I was convinced that the principles of the Fund for Humanity could work anywhere. The determining factor, I assured Birdie, is not geography or population density; it is trust in God and faithful adherence to the economics of Jesus.

Like many other dedicated Christians I know, Birdie Lytle seems to have enough energy for about three people. And one letter of encouragement from Zaire was all that was needed. Birdie was off and running.

Months later, when Linda and I were back in the United States, I learned the details of the initial get-together, in Birdie's living room, of what would eventually become the San Antonio Habitat Committee.

Birdie had assembled ten interested people, and a diverse

bunch of Christians they were. In addition to Presbyterians Birdie and Bill, there were Marcia and Charlie Hare, a young Methodist couple who had been seeking ways to put their faith into action; Mary Emeny, who had recently worked with the American Friends Service Committee in Vietnam, and Hunter Ingalls, her art history-professor husband; Rod and Patti Radle, a couple of Roman Catholic background who voluntarily lived with their family in poverty in order to serve the people of west-side San Antonio; and two other Catholics, Bob Galvan, a civil service worker at Kelly Air Force Base, and Brother Fred, an engineer and an indefatigable worker whom both the Lytles described as "a St. Francis sort of man."

It was a spring evening in 1976. The time grew later and later as these ten friends debated and discussed at length what they might be able to do about housing for the poor in San Antonio. But despite the hour, their eagerness kept growing. They would begin! They would step out in faith, depending on the Lord for direction and support.

Before the group separated for the night, they all huddled on the floor around a spread-out map of San Antonio.

"We'll start over here on the west side. Later on, we can move over to the east side—conditions there are just as bad."

"Right! We can build little oases of decent housing all over the city!"

"If it can work in Georgia and Zaire, it can work here!"

Then the dreamers, wondering a little what they had gotten themselves in for, settled down to the practical nitty-gritty of organizing the first Fund for Humanity in a large U.S. city. Initially they decided that the geographical focus for the Fund would be Inner City Development, a neighborhood center on the corner of Trinity and Chihuahua run by Rod and Patti Radle. The recreational and enrichment programs there had already won the confidence of the local people, and Inner City was a center for the distribution of emergency food and clothing. The need for decent shelter in that neighborhood was just as desperate.

The committee had no money. But they plunged ahead

anyway. By fall the San Antonio Fund for Humanity was incorporated—an independent, nonprofit group which would later affiliate with the new organization of Habitat for Humanity, Inc. They elected an official board of directors and began fund raising; an initial gift of $1,950 from one committed director was already in the bank.

At the next meeting another map was laid out on the floor for study. It showed odd pieces of ground the city had put up for sale.

"Folks, we need to make a bid on one of these lots—the deadline is Thursday." Bob Galvan was urging the board members to act quickly, and there wasn't time to visit the location in question.

"Look, let's go ahead on faith. Here's a lot the right size, and it's in our target area. What'll we bid?"

"Well. . . . It's the bicentennial year, but $1,776 is too much. How about $1,376? That's in the realm of the going price, I think."

The bid was placed—and promptly accepted. A lot on Hidalgo Street belonged to the new San Antonio Fund for Humanity, Inc.

Then the board went out to study their newly acquired real estate. To their dismay, the 60-by-75-foot lot turned out to have a wide, broken trail of thick cement, the remains of a driveway, covering one entire side and running all across the back as well. How could they ever afford to remove all this concrete, in order to lay a foundation?

The Lord had the answer, as always. Brother Jim Jackley, from nearby St. Mary's University, donated a Caterpillar earth mover, spent one full day manipulating it on that lot from 8 A.M. till dusk, and completely disposed of the cement problem.

The venture proceeded in this way. For each new difficulty there was a corresponding solution to be found—though it often took a lot of patient and prayerful searching.

The biggest problems, of course, were financial. The board worked up a slide/tape show about the project and took it to any church or organization that would give them a hearing.

Before long, a few families became interested enough to pledge a regular 10 percent of their own house payments to the Fund. A realtor began giving 10 percent of his commissions, and one church decided to schedule a special annual offering. Skilled volunteers donated large chunks of time without pay. A nucleus of support was growing.

Another problem had to be dealt with differently. Hidalgo Street, the board members were told by apprehensive residents, was the worst one in the area; there had been murders on that street in recent years. Children on nearby blocks called Hidalgo "the Devil's Triangle" and avoided walking there. There was only one thing to do: rename the area, as we had done earlier when Bokotola became Losanganya. So the Devil's Triangle became, for the Habitat people, "the Triangle of the Father, Son, and Holy Spirit"—and the work continued.

As more supporters joined the group, a family selection committee was formed, and Ernesto and Sylvia Torres and their four children were chosen to receive the first house. The Torres family lived in a nearby three-room shack. The bathroom consisted of a toilet in a closet, and large cracks around the crooked kitchen door allowed winter winds to blow right through the rooms. But Ernesto, a painter, worked hard to make this ramshackle dwelling as livable as possible, and Sylvia somehow kept it spotless. The Torreses were thrilled to become the Fund's first family, and they pitched in to work every available minute at the site.

The Lord provided an excellent local contractor, Richard Villasana (whose name means "healthy town"!), and he obtained materials at the best possible cost. As work crews and the Torres family and volunteers met week after week at the lot on Hidalgo Street, relationships were being built—along with an attractive, three-bedroom brick-veneer home. On October 21, 1978, a large crowd of friends and neighbors gathered at the site for a picnic and a memorable ceremony of house blessing.

The cost of this first home was $16,700. The Torres family made a down payment of $400, and their monthly payments are $50 for the house and $35 for taxes, insurance, and utilities. After they moved in, Ernesto and Sylvia kept improving their property, adding an attractive fence, grass, trees, and flowers. They continued to attend meetings of the Fund, and Ernesto volunteered his painting skills on the second house. This one, a block and a half away on a slightly larger lot, was planned with four bedrooms—for the Espinosa family of ten children. Ground was broken for this house in January 1980.

It took four years of hard work for the San Antonio Fund for Humanity to become organized, raise funds, purchase lots, and build the first two houses. During this process, all the people involved learned that the positive things which were happening within themselves and their city were more significant than how fast they were able to complete how many houses. As Birdie says, "We have come to realize that God's timing is always right."

It will be exciting to see what He has next on His schedule for San Antonio.

1

2

3

1 In 1968, the Millard Fuller family, rejecting their former life of affluence, moved into a second-floor apartment at Koinonia Farm, a Christian community near Americus, Georgia.
2 They also left behind their fancy cars, and on the farm they used simpler transportation. (From left: Millard with Faith, Kim, Linda, and Chris.)
3 The idea of building homes for poor people began in discussions with the late biblical scholar and author Clarence Jordan, founder of Koinonia Farm.

4 

5 

6 

4 The desperate state of local housing was a matter of deep concern among Koinonia residents.
5 In 1969, Koinonia Partners laid out forty-two home sites on the farm for local families, and the first home was begun for the happy new owners, Bo and Emma Johnson.
6 Since then, the project has expanded into the town of Americus, where dismal shacks like these are being removed.

7

8

9

7 These solid dwellings are replacing the shacks. Houses are sold at cost with a small down payment. Purchasers carry a twenty-year, *no-interest* mortgage.
8 In 1973, the Fullers took the Koinonia Partners concept of community building to Zaire, Africa, and began work to replace some of the squalid housing in the city of Mbandaka. (See Chapter 7.)
9 Lokoba, one of the local workmen, began digging the foundation for the first house in Mbandaka in March 1974. Note the church in the distance.

10

11

12

10 All the work for these homes was done by hand. Here the builders lift a lintel into place.
11 And here two of the Fuller girls, Faith and Georgia, help with the house painting.
12 In just two years, many homes were complete and occupied. This photo was taken in March 1976 from the same spot as Photo #9 was taken. Note the church in the background. Other construction included a park, a community center, and the only playground for the Mbandaka population of 150,000 people.

13

14

13 The excitement of the home-building program in Mbandaka spread to the little jungle village of Ntondo, ninety miles away, where a bold plan was launched to rebuild the whole community—300 new homes! (See Chapter 1.) To move supplies, people, and groceries, Habitat for Humanity bought a dump truck.
14 Habitat volunteer Dana Rominger raised funds in his home church in North Carolina to replace this crumbling mud-brick hut that housed a family of fourteen. (See Chapter 13.)

15

16

17

15 Then he went to Ntondo for two months to work with these community members to build the new house.
16 As their home neared completion in January 1979, both the family of Nkanga Mpolo and volunteer Rominger experienced great joy.
17 By the middle of 1980, more than 150 new homes were finished or under way in Ntondo.

18

18 Workers in eleven nearby villages also are laboriously making cement blocks in hopes of starting their own building projects.

19 Outside the teeming capital city of Kinshasa in Zaire, a new building project was launched in 1979 under the direction of a local Habitat for Humanity committee of Americans and Zairois. (See Chapter 12. From left: Leon Emmert, Pastor Lubuimi, Cliff Stabell, Kilola, Malonga, Madeata, Moni, and Ngonda.)

19

20 

21 

22 

20 Volunteer architect Chuck Clark went out to the site near Kinshasa to survey land for 130 homes, a church, a school, a clinic, two parks, and two market areas. With him are community workers assisting in the project.
21 As the Kinshasa houses began to go up, hundreds of applications poured in from needy families.
22 This beaming father holds a card indicating that his family has been selected to receive one of the first houses.

23

23 A Habitat for Humanity committee was organized in San Antonio, Texas, in 1976. At that time, the Ernesto Torres family of six lived in this rented shack. (See Chapter 9.)

24 Today the Torres family owns this solid new home, built with funds raised locally by the San Antonio committee.

24

25

26

27

25 The Espinoza family, with ten children, eagerly took part in the groundbreaking for the second San Antonio house in January 1980.

26 In Immokalee, Florida, volunteer Larry Stoner helps build Habitat housing for migrant workers. (See Chapter 12.)

27 When the first families were chosen to live in the new homes, a picnic was held at the Immokalee site. Volunteers Bob and Amy Olsen are seated in the front row at left and at right.

8

29

30

28 Like all homeowners in the Immokalee project, Juan Garcia and his family are contributing 2,000 hours of labor.
29 Today the Garcia family lives in this first house.
30 Louis Spencer and Danny Bachelor work on the roof of Samuel Gadsden's house. All these families are receiving new homes.

31 

32 

33 

31 Millard Fuller was guest speaker at the dedication service for the first three Immokalee houses in February 1980.
32 In Appalachia, the Habitat Committee for Morgan and Scott counties in Tennessee selected the John and Mary Hawn family to receive the first house. John Hawn worked on the building crew. (See Chapter 10.)
33 The Hawns moved into their solid new home in the spring of 1979.

34 The Habitat for Humanity idea keeps spreading. Another hardworking committee has obtained land in Kansas City, Missouri. In October 1979, they held their first groundbreaking. (See Chapter 14.)
35 In Fort Myers, Florida, a local Habitat committee is working to replace houses like this in the "Harlem Heights" section of town.
36 On February 23, 1980, committee members and prospective homeowners attended a groundbreaking ceremony on donated land in Fort Myers.

37

38

39

37 In Tucson, Arizona, a Habitat committee has picked two target areas in the city where they are working to eliminate housing like this.
38 In Beaumont, Texas, when the Habitat committee obtained their first piece of land, they held a picnic with neighbors to dedicate the site.
39 In the village of Aguacatan in the Central American country of Guatemala, fifty-three impoverished families have banded together to begin a Habitat housing project. (See Chapter 12.)

40

40 Volunteer Bob Stevens helps one of the villagers make soil-cement blocks in a form.

41 One at a time, the blocks are pressed out and laid in the sun to dry.

41

42 

 4

44 

42 The Aguacatan villagers have always lived in houses of sticks and cornstalks, sometimes with polyethylene sheets stretched over frames for protection from the wind.
43 Now they are building solid new homes for themselves, complete with steel reinforcing rods to resist earthquakes.
44 The Millard Fuller family today. (From left: Kim, Georgia, Linda, Millard, Faith, and Chris.)

10

Another Step: Appalachia

A few months after Linda and I had returned from Zaire, we were visited by three young pastors from Tennessee and their wives. They represented the Morgan-Scott Project, an ecumenical effort named for the two rural counties it serves. For five years, this project, supported by eight different Christian groups, had worked through programs—including health care, tutoring, legal assistance, and senior citizens' groups—to aid low-income residents of this section of Appalachia.

One of the greatest needs in their area, we learned, was housing. The project had already done some work on home repairs, but almost 40 percent of the houses in Morgan and Scott counties had been classified as substandard, as opposed to an average of 17 percent throughout the state.

Would the Habitat concept work, they asked, in the hills of Tennessee? By the time we had talked and shared with our guests for several hours, they had made up their minds. They returned home fired up to try. That was in January of 1977.

"For the next year we fumbled around, trying to figure out how to fit Habitat into the programs we already had going," said Mark Frey, one of our visitors. At that time Mark was serving as lay pastor of two United Church of Christ congregations with about twenty members each, in addition to his involvement with the Morgan-Scott ministry. "But then the Lord began to drop things in our lap to get us moving."

On December 30, 1977, a local businessman came to see Bob Butziger, the Presbyterian pastor who headed the Morgan-Scott Project.

"I've just arranged to sell a parcel of ninety-three acres along Alice Creek," the man said. "When the deal looked settled, someone decided to renege on a piece that's about eighteen acres. I've heard you people are looking for land, and if you can come up with the money before the end of the year, I'll sell it to you for $5,500."

Before the end of the year—the next day was New Year's Eve! Most of the fledgling Habitat committee had gone away for the Christmas holidays. Besides, they had no money.

But this was the Lord's project. Within less than the required two days, Bob had checked out the piece of ground, the Morgan-Scott directors had agreed to advance the cash to the Fund for Humanity, and eighteen acres of beautiful wooded property had been acquired at a bargain price.

Shortly thereafter, a young man came to Mark Frey to ask Mark to perform his wedding. As the pastor and the engaged couple got acquainted, Mark asked the prospective groom about his occupation.

"I'm a surveyor."

A surveyor!

"I did a pretty good job with that wedding," Mark said, "and I also told the man what we were hoping to do for the local people through the Habitat project. He got really interested, and since then he has carefully surveyed our whole eighteen acres, charging us nothing for his time. We laid out nine home sites, leaving wooded areas between to be cut for fuel. This spacing would also avoid other potential problems; mountain families might feel uncomfortably squeezed in on smaller lots.

"We started with twelve people working on the building

portion of Habitat. At our first crew meeting I reminded everyone that Jesus started with the same number and that maybe God had called us together specifically to witness to His love in this small part of Tennessee.

"We chose the first family, John and Mary Hawn and their four children, when we had just $1,500 in the bank. At that time John was about to head for Nashville, 180 miles away, to look for work. We hired him for the Habitat building crew, and he really pitched in."

John Hawn and his wife had been paying rent of $30 a month for a tumbledown house with no water. A year later, thanks to gifts to the Morgan-Scott Fund for Humanity that came in from all over the country, the Hawn family moved into the first new home at the Alice Creek site.

The Hawns' three-bedroom house cost $16,000, including the 1.9-acre lot. After a down payment of $250, their monthly payments are $68 over twenty years, plus $15 monthly property taxes. Furthermore, John found employment with a private contractor after his work on the building crew—so he acquired both a decent home and good job through Habitat for Humanity.

With the Hawns' house barely completed, the Habitat committee (on which John Hawn continued to serve as an active member) began construction on two more houses. One is on a neighboring lot to the Hawns' in Morgan County, and the other is located in next-door Scott County. The Hawns' house payments gave the Fund for Humanity a small monthly boost, and other support somehow kept coming in as the work proceeded. Concerning the whole effort, Mark Frey told us, "We're not even sure what we need sometimes, but the Lord keeps providing anyway!"

There are many amazing Christians on the Morgan-Scott Habitat committee. One of them is Vickie Preston. Although her own family's income is subsistence level, Vickie came up with ideas for church rummage sales and bake sales and a car wash to raise funds for Habitat for Humanity. The fact that all these affairs put together netted a total donation of just $100 is some indication of the limited cash resources of many people in that part of our country. Vickie's beautiful gift represented tremendous dedication and hard work.

But I haven't told you the most important aspect of Vickie's idea. She was so full of excitement about sharing God's love through Habitat that she organized all these events *to raise funds for the building projects in Zaire!*

It is this spirit—this incredible love overflowing all economic, racial, and national barriers—which makes Habitat work.

Anywhere.

11
A House in Americus

When the new organization called Habitat for Humanity decided in the fall of 1976 that it needed a headquarters in the town of Americus, I also needed a law office. I had passed the Georgia bar exams before leaving for Zaire, and now that I was no longer a full-time missionary, I had to find some means of feeding my family. So I began looking for an inexpensive building in the area where Linda and I could work on Habitat correspondence in one room and legal papers in another.

What I didn't know was that this need, too, had been taken care of by the Lord years before.

Back in 1971, a youth group from a church in Andalusia, Alabama, came to Koinonia for a week of work and study. I was impressed with the pastor, Jim Jackson, as we shared in discussions about Biblical imperatives for Christian living.

Before the work campers departed, Jim asked me to come and speak at his church. I hesitated, reminding him that my appearance might create problems, since I could not accept any limitations on who could come with me or what I could talk about.

Jim assured me that I would be free to preach as the Spirit led, and we set a date. I was to speak three times—in Sunday school, in the worship service, and again on Sunday evening.

Several weeks later, Linda and I set out for Andalusia on a Saturday afternoon. The drive took about four hours. On the way, Linda discovered that she had torn her stockings, and we stopped in the little town of Luverne, Alabama, to get another pair.

As we stepped out of the car, we immediately bumped into a black friend from Luverne, James Kolb. In fact, just a month earlier, Mr. Kolb had invited me to come to Luverne to preach in his church, and I had enjoyed a fine day with his congregation.

"Goodness, Mr. Fuller," he greeted me. "What you doin' back in Luverne today?"

"We're on our way to Andalusia. I'm speaking tomorrow at the First Congregational Church."

"Man, that's a white church. How'd you get invited to speak there?"

"Well, the minister spent a week at Koinonia recently. Say, why don't you come down tomorrow, too?"

"Would they let me come in?"

"If they won't, I'll leave. But the minister assured me that everyone will be welcome."

"Okay, I'd like to come. I'll check with my wife, and I hope we'll see you in the morning."

By this time, Linda had returned from purchasing her stockings. We shook hands with Mr. Kolb and continued on our way.

That night I told Jim Jackson about our encounter with our friend in Luverne, and about the possibility that he would visit the church on Sunday. Jim appeared to have no qualms.

"That's fine," he said. "I hope he comes."

The next morning I spoke to a large group of adults in Sunday school and met a friendly reception. As the eleven o'clock service began, there was no sign of Mr. Kolb. Perhaps something had come up, after all.

At about eleven-fifteen, we were singing the second hymn,

"In Christ There Is No East or West," which Jim had carefully chosen for the message I wanted to present. The congregation had just begun the third verse:

> Join hands, then, brothers of the faith,
> Whate'er your race may be;
> Who serves my Father as a son
> Is surely kin to Me.

Into the rear of the church walked James Kolb, his wife, and his teenage daughter. They came quietly down the center aisle about halfway and chose an empty pew. As I surveyed the congregation from the pulpit, I saw some nervous glances and a few stares, but no panic. No one got up and left.

The service continued, and I delivered the sermon, not forgetting to emphasize the oneness of God's children, whatever their race or social standing. After the benediction there were some parishioners who ducked out quickly, but others stayed to shake hands and chat with us and the Kolb family.

The "parsonage" for Jim Jackson, his wife Sheila, and their two children was their mobile home, which was parked right next door to the church. They invited the Kolbs to stay for lunch, along with Linda and me, and the nine of us ended up talking happily all afternoon. That evening, I returned to the church to talk to a youth meeting, and the Kolbs also came, with their daughter.

All the way back to Koinonia on Monday, Linda and I talked about what a fine time we had enjoyed in Andalusia, how smoothly the services had gone, and what a historic moment that all-white church had experienced. We couldn't get over the appropriateness of the Kolbs' arrival during that hymn, and the friendliness with which they had been received.

On Monday evening we had a phone call from Jim Jackson. Following an emergency meeting of his board of deacons, he had just been fired. This action was taken, he had been told, not just because he had brought blacks into the church, although that was bad enough, but also because he had staged this invasion so blatantly, during a particular verse of a specially chosen hymn!

The deacons wanted the Jacksons to leave immediately. Before the week was out, the family had pulled their mobile home to Koinonia, where they stayed and worked for about a year. Andalusia was Jim Jackson's third and last pastorate.

In 1972, Jim took his small savings and bought a modest house at 417 West Church Street in Americus. It was right at the edge of a divided neighborhood—mostly poor blacks in one direction and middle-income whites in the other. From this base, Jim and Sheila operated a sort of unpaid community ministry to underprivileged children. They did a lot of tutoring and counseling and even embarked on a summer camp program. When we left for Africa in 1973, it was the Jacksons who drove us to the airport. By the time we returned three years later, however, the Jackson family had moved to a new job in Oregon, and we could keep in touch only through correspondence.

One Sunday in late 1976, I was chatting with a friend before a church service in Americus. At that point I was actively searching for quarters for my law/Habitat office, but nothing had turned up. Suddenly our conversation became more than casual.

"When Jim Jackson moved out West," she was saying, "he left it up to me to sell that house of theirs. Last week I was sure I had it sold, but then the deal fell through."

A bell rang in my head. I jotted down all the information Jim's friend had about the house and wrote him a letter that same afternoon. Jim responded promptly, and shortly thereafter he sold me the house for $4,000. We tore off the decaying front porch and replaced it with a smaller one, adding a wide brick walkway and steps. Linda took on the chore of stripping layers of paint from the old front door, sanding and refinishing it to complete an attractive entranceway. She also replaced broken windows, put up shelves, made drapes, and scoured local secondhand shops for furnishings. Then we applied fresh exterior paint over the old clapboards, and we had our office building.

Shortly thereafter, our family moved from Koinonia to another house on Church Street a few blocks from the Habitat office. Linda was able to continue her invaluable partnership in Habitat's ministry, handling mountains of typing and correspondence, often working nights and weekends, and at the same time being very much a full-time mother. And, although it was never their favorite occupation, we even managed occasionally to draft our children onto the envelope-stuffing crew.

More recently, Habitat has been able to purchase the house next door to our office, and several other houses on the same block. One at a time, we have renovated and painted these dwellings with volunteer help and furnished them with the assistance of the Goodwill store. While we have been acquiring much-needed office space for Habitat and sleeping quarters for visitors and volunteers, the neighborhood has begun to display a fresh, spruced-up look that was equally needed.

One of our acquisitions near the Habitat office was a half-acre lot containing two dilapidated shacks. We proceeded to repair the first one inside and out, working carefully around the elderly wheelchair-bound man who lived there. The second dwelling was completely hopeless. So we built a small cement block house in front of it, and then a visiting work camp group knocked down the old heap of rotting boards. Now the retired couple who delightedly moved out of their rickety shack into a solid home are using the wood from their old house to heat the new one. Both households continue to pay Habitat the same amount they paid the former owner: $40 and $15 per month, respectively.

As I sit here in Jim and Sheila Jackson's former home in Americus and labor over this manuscript, I sometimes wonder where I might be working now if Jim had never invited me to preach at his church in Andalusia. But then, Jim probably wonders the same thing about himself.

12
The Experiment Expands

As more and more people learned about the Habitat for Humanity concept, it began to spread in exciting ways.

In a small town in southwestern Florida, the Church of the Brethren operated an emergency food and clothing assistance program for migrant farm workers called Immokalee Neighborhood Services, Inc. Ironically, the town's name comes from a Seminole Indian word meaning "my home"—and that's one thing that is completely out of reach of most migrant workers.

But in 1978 four volunteers came together in Immokalee to contribute their energies and expertise toward launching a Habitat housing project. Bob Olsen, a retired engineering professor from Penn State, and his wife Amy were supported by the Brethren Volunteer Services, and Larry and Karen Stoner volunteered under the Eastern Mennonite Board of Missions and Charities. Larry was an experienced builder who had worked with us before, first at Koinonia for two and a half years and then for two and a half more years in Zaire. In fact, at age twenty-seven, Larry was already being referred to around our office as the "senior Habitat person"!

Thanks to the leadership of these four energetic and talented Christians, a Fund for Humanity was inaugurated in Immokalee, and committee members began to contact churches in the area for support. In the fall of 1978 the Fund made a 10-percent down payment—because that was all the cash there was—on five acres of land, in complete faith that by December 1, the final settlement date, the other 90 percent of the money would come from somewhere. The funds did come, and in time.

Gradually, new homes began to go up. The dream of the planners of the Immokalee project was to complete a Christian community of perhaps 160 acres with homes for sixty families. The project would be equally divided among black, Spanish-speaking, and Anglo residents, and it would include a community building, recreation facilities, and even opportunities for rainy-day employment.

Getting the dream moving toward reality was slow and difficult—both the construction itself, and the fund raising that had to precede each step. But by early 1980 two of the first three houses were completed, and their elated new owners had moved in. In February of that year I participated in a moving service held at the Immokalee building site, dedicating these first three houses to God. Each of the families—one black, one white, one of Mexican descent—had made a down payment of $500 on their three- or four-bedroom homes, which cost approximately $20,000. The families were also required to contribute a minimum of 2,000 hours of labor, thereby increasing their personal commitment to the success of the project. As their monthly payments of $100 began to come back into the Fund, the money was quickly recycled into more building materials for more houses.

While the project was still in its early stages, the Lord provided a unique fund-raising opportunity for the Immokalee committee.

Right in the center of the city of Naples, forty-five miles west of Immokalee on the Gulf of Mexico, there was a five-acre ghetto where 167 people were crammed into eighty-three wretched shacks. (In Immokalee, nine homes had been planned for the same amount of land.) Raw sewage, trash, and dead animals surrounded a shambles of rotting buildings, and the area had understandably been declared "unfit for human habitation."

Even the name—"McDonald's Quarters"—had connotations of misery; it referred to the time when slaves had been quartered on this property. Yet just a few blocks from these shacks stood spacious developments of high-rise apartments and plush and imposing single-family dwellings. Naples is reported to have more than 600 millionaires among its population.

The entire McDonald's Quarters area had been condemned and was about to be razed. But there was absolutely no place for the residents to go—and a planned government housing project for the city was at least a year and a half in the future. In July of 1979, when the Immokalee project was, as usual, nearly out of funds, some concerned citizens of Naples approached the Habitat committee with a proposal.

"If we can raise the estimated $70,000 it will cost to bring those houses into conformation with the building codes," the citizens asked, "will you take on the job? We can negotiate a contract with the landlord so that, when repairs are completed, all subsequent rent money will go into the Fund for Humanity."

The Habitat board members, many of them migrant farm workers, debated that large question. The renovations would be an enormous task, and possibly their efforts in Immokalee would be slowed. On the other hand, as one member pointed out, "We're here to help poor people, and they sure are poor in the Quarters!" In the end, the board voted overwhelmingly to go ahead, and the Lord blessed their efforts.

The Circuit Court judge postponed his demolition order just three days before it was scheduled to be carried out.

The committee of concerned citizens raised *more* than the promised $70,000 for repairs.

A local company donated 300 gallons of house paint; another provided fifteen new windows.

A roofing firm completely replaced one roof ($1,800) at no charge.

An exterminator volunteered to treat every dwelling for roaches when the work was finished.

The county health department decided to hold a clinic in the renovated central building, which had formerly been a notorious bar, and in the evenings and on Sunday, a local church began to hold services there.

Finally, in true Habitat fashion, McDonald's Quarters was officially renamed. It is now Progress Village.

By December 1, 1979, seventy-eight houses had been completely repaired; the other five were deemed hopeless and had to be torn down. The yards were cleared of debris, and the homes were freshly painted. Five different city inspectors (building, plumbing, electrical wiring, sanitation, and fire) had approved every dwelling. The members of the building crew which had been detailed to Naples (including one Catholic sister) returned to the Immokalee project. And the rent payments, which had not been made for months, were coming into the Immokalee Fund for Humanity at the rate of $1,000 per week.

The Habitat committee had contracted to continue management of the village through 1980. For at least one year, even as 167 people were living for the first time in decent housing in Naples, their rent money would be helping to build still more homes in Immokalee.

The entire effort in Naples received excellent coverage in the news media, and I especially appreciated one article which appeared in the *Miami Herald* on October 6, 1979. It referred to the newly emerging Progress Village area as a "born-again slum." I cannot imagine a better three-word description of a Habitat project.

On John's Island, off the coast of South Carolina, there is no real industry, and many local families have no employment other than seasonal farm work. For ten years, from 1969 to 1979, the Eastern Mennonite Board of Missions and Charities had operated a Voluntary Service Unit on this small (fifteen miles long) island. The volunteers, who stayed for terms of from six months to two years and worked for room and board and $20 a month, provided health and day-care services for local residents and made Band-Aid kinds of repairs on their desperately poor shacks.

But the Mennonites kept looking for ways to become more significantly involved with local needs. They had long been sending us volunteer builders, first to Koinonia and later also to Zaire. After Habitat for Humanity had been officially constituted, the John's Island group began to explore the possibility of launching a home-building project there in affiliation with this new organization.

In October of 1979 the foundation was laid for the first Habitat house on John's Island. Actually, the Mennonites had purchased a ten-acre plot of land back in 1976, but construction had been stymied during the intervening years by endless foul-ups with various governmental agencies. The volunteers never gave up, however, and the prayers and gifts of many interested people, distant friends as well as those on the scene, never stopped. By Christmas of 1979 the first house was under roof, and another small community of hope was on its way to becoming a reality.

Meanwhile, we kept getting requests from Zaire for more housing projects. Church groups in every region of that country wanted advice and assistance in building homes for the poor.

Probably the worst living conditions in all of Zaire exist in the teeming (population 2.5 million) capital city of Kinshasa. When a worker (if he can find employment) earning an average of $75 per month has to pay $3 for a pound of sugar and $6 for a pound of the cheapest meat, he can scarcely afford to feed his family, let alone obtain suitable housing. It was here in Kinshasa that the leaders of the Zairois church decided to start next. American Baptists, who had done extensive mission work in this area, agreed in 1978 to provide seed money to launch a Habitat project in the capital city under the leadership of Cliff and Joy Stabell of Illinois, longtime Baptist missionaries to Zaire. They were soon joined by Clive

Rainey, a Southern Baptist volunteer from Americus, Georgia.

Inevitably, months of bureaucratic confusion followed. One day I heard Linda sitting at her desk in the Habitat office, chuckling aloud. When I investigated, I discovered that she was reading the latest letter from Cliff Stabell in Zaire, and his tale was one with which we ourselves were all too familiar. He had sent a diary of one month's efforts recounting a ludicrous succession of fruitless marches he had made from one government office to the next. Every bureaucrat in Kinshasa, it seemed, thought the proposed Habitat project was indeed a fine idea—and not one was ever available to expedite anything.

But the Lord was still at work. Finally, in the summer of 1979, a complete new community was begun on a 115-acre hillside a few miles outside the capital. Chuck Clark, the young Atlanta architect who planned and built the park in Mbandaka in 1975, and who laid out the fifty-six-house extension there, volunteered to return to Zaire to survey the new site in Kinshasa. Eventually this plot of land, which was donated by the government, will hold 130 houses, a church, a school, a clinic, two parks, and two market areas. By early 1980, the first 20 of these houses were already under construction, with several of them complete and occupied. And because of its location near a crowded urban area, the Kinshasa development will be a particularly visible witness to Christ's love translated into action, serving His people in need.*

In April of 1979 the Habitat Board of Directors, the fantastic ecumenical group which guides Habitat for Humanity, voted to take a step of faith in a new direction.

In a tiny Indian village in the Guatemalan highlands called

---

* The Kinshasa project was the first step toward carrying out a mandate voted by the National Synod of the Church of Christ in Zaire to extend Habitat projects throughout the country. Pastor Bokeleale, president of the Church of Christ in Zaire, wrote me about that action in a letter dated August 15, 1977: "I have just returned from our National Synod which was held in Kasai and I must inform you officially that it voted for the project to be extended everywhere, in every region of Zaire. Thus, we have a great responsibility! It concerns not just Mbandaka and Ntondo, but the whole Republic. I hope to discusss with you how to meet this great need for I can see that Habitat for Humanity must undertake the complete experiment in Zaire, which will be an example for other countries."

Aguacatan, a group of fifty-three families had organized themselves some years earlier in an effort to improve their subsistence-level existence. The villagers were barely surviving by raising corn and beans on plots ranging from one-half acre to seven or eight acres and by laboring in nearby garlic fields for about $1.50 per day. A few migrated seasonally to the coast to work on the cotton, coffee, or sugarcane harvests. Banding together, the families had inaugurated a small beekeeping cooperative through Heifer Project, and they solicited a latrine construction program through the Guatemalan government. But their efforts to obtain decent housing had come to nothing.

Now, under the leadership of the Reverend Bob Stevens, an engineer-sociologist-pastor with many years of experience in Latin America, Habitat decided to undertake a fifty-three-unit development in Aguacatan to replace the existing shantytown of mud, cornstalk, and tin houses. The simple two- or three-bedroom homes would be built of soil-cement block with reinforced walls and beams for earthquake resistance; they would have corrugated iron roofing. With the community supplying the labor, the cost per unit was figured at about $1,150 plus $150 for each well. Another $200 per family was allocated for agricultural and nutritional programs and for backyard industries.

For a total of $1,500, the standard of living of an entire family could be dramatically and permanently transformed. At the end of 1979, as the first homes began to go up in Aguacatan, Habitat volunteers and villagers were enthusiastically working together toward that transformation.

During that same year, groups of people representing a wide spectrum of Christian faiths were gathering in Kansas City, Missouri; Denver, Colorado; Beaumont, Texas; Fort Myers, Florida; Tucson, Arizona; and Paducah, Kentucky. In each city there evolved an ecumenical committee that determined to tackle local housing problems in affiliation with Habitat for Humanity.

Acquiring land in the inner city is often difficult. The red tape of zoning laws and building codes can be maddening, and securing a clear title is sometimes virtually impossible due to missing heirs or absentee landowners. And when construction finally does begin, the constant, nagging need for more funds provides another inescapable lesson in patience! But each one of these projects is moving ahead, and even as this book is being written, we are receiving inquiries from other locations where Christians want to become involved in putting love in the mortar joints.

It is important to realize that every Habitat project is operated independently by its own local board of directors. This board must include representation from sponsoring church groups, volunteers working on the project, and families who are eligible to receive homes. The manner of selecting the families, and the wording of their contracts, may vary somewhat from place to place, but every project is conducted within general Habitat guidelines.

For example, although we accept, and even solicit, grants of government land and the installation of streets and water systems, we do not seek government money to finance Habitat's houses. Rather, they must be a tangible witness to the basic Biblical responsibility which every Christian has to share with a brother or sister in need. And even though no interest is ever charged, these homes are not a "giveaway." On the contrary. Habitat projects do not even distinguish between "givers" and "receivers." Christ teaches that it is more blessed to give—and in the Habitat concept everyone, rich and poor and in between, can do so. The humblest family that receives a home will continue to be giving, through their house payments and contributions of labor, and they are encouraged, if they possibly can, to donate to the Fund *in addition to* their house payments, to help another family as they have been helped.

The fledgling Habitat committee in Denver provided us with a beautiful witness to this kind of sharing. While they were still struggling to become established, before their first lot had been acquired, they began tithing their funds to Habitat. That is, they regularly sent to the office in Americus one tenth of whatever money they raised, in order to strengthen other projects!

Another example of this over-and-above giving took place at the July 1979 dedication service in Ntondo. Before we left, the Habitat committee there presented me with half the $400 offering which had been received that day, to be sent to the new building project in an impoverished village in Guatemala that I had just told them about. The chances are that none of the 3,000 Africans present at that service, themselves mostly very poor, will ever visit Aguacatan, Guatemala. But their gift will go in their stead, and they will surely receive a rich blessing from this act of sacrificial sharing.

A primary factor in all Habitat projects is the concept of *partnership.* Respect for customs and cultural values is paramount. On overseas projects, volunteers attempt to become fluent in the language, and they are encouraged to live in the homes of local families whenever possible. The building of relationships that takes place as people share life with each other is just as significant and valuable as the more tangible house building that they are accomplishing at the same time.

A concern for the total needs of persons is always present. A Habitat project may include space for a playground, a community center, vegetable gardens, backyard industries—the demands of each situation determine the planning. Technological developments introduced by Habitat must be economical and environmentally sound—adobe bricks in Denver, a solar wall in Tennessee, cement-shingle "Habitile" roofs in Zaire.

Whatever the local considerations, a Habitat for Humanity project is always operated as a demonstration plot of love in action. It is evangelistic, simultaneously incarnating and verbalizing the Gospel. And when the Lord is the most important One in any venture, it will succeed.

As we entered the 1980s, hundreds of houses for families in need had been built under these principles in fourteen locations, beginning at Koinonia in Georgia in 1968. In each of these areas, money from gifts and noninterest loans and partnership industries and house payments continues to come in to the local Fund for Humanity, and construction is proceeding. The families' payments are generally up to date, and some are paid ahead. Mbomba, our energetic work foreman in Mbandaka (who first came to the project as a penniless, unemployed laborer), completed his twenty-year mortgage obligation in just three years.

And we have never, in any project, had to make a foreclosure.

13
The Volunteers

Goleta, California
January 6, 1978

Dear Habitat for Humanity:

I have been telling God for several years now that I wanted to serve Him in the way that I think Christians ought to serve: with hands, mouth, and purse. I have investigated several kinds of ministries; two of these have extended invitations. . . .

Last night I began reading *Bokotola* and I could not set it down until I had finished. . . . I am in complete agreement with the policy of Habitat for Humanity in their approach toward Christian community development. I would like very much to be a part of your ministry in Zaire. As I stated earlier, I have prayed for this kind of opportunity, and if I were to become involved in Habitat, it would be an answer to my prayers.

I have my passport and International Health Card. . . . I will be in New York on business about the 15th of February. If things progress favorably, it may be that I could continue on from there.

With sincere Christian regards,

Kenneth E. Harris

A few weeks after we received this letter, Ken Harris, an American Baptist who had learned of Habitat through Lutheran World Ministries, was en route to Zaire. Ken, a Stanford Ed.D. (Doctor of Education), had recently retired from the U.S. Agency for International Development with years of overseas experience behind him. His practical skills included farming, construction, and furniture making.

For six months during 1978, Ken worked at the project in Mbandaka, covering all his own expenses and sharing his expertise in wonderful ways. Since his return to the States, Ken has served as a construction consultant on technical problems for Habitat, and he has been an effective fundraiser for new equipment at the Mbandaka project.

Dale Long, a Mennonite from Lancaster County, Pennsylvania, spent two years in Zaire contributing his skills in the field of agriculture. Combining a college degree in biology with a love of working outdoors, Dale labored to improve the dismal diets of impoverished Zairois families. Their staple foods are *kwanga* (manioc roots, which have little nutritional value and which must be soaked in a swamp for a week to remove the poisonous acid content) and *pondu* (manioc leaves), supplemented occasionally by fish, chicken, monkey, or goat meat.

In cooperation with six international agricultural agencies, Dale introduced in the village of Ntondo some new, larger peanuts from Florida, high-lysine tropical corn from Mexico, black beans from Puerto Rico, cowpeas and celosia from Nigeria, pigeonpeas and sunflowers from India, tomatoes from Taiwan, and papayas from Hawaii. He even packed 300 citrus seedlings in a big picnic cooler and took them along to Zaire by plane. Never mind that the airline lost his luggage. It turned up a week later; Dale planted the seedlings, and many survived to become a small citrus nursery.

Dale met constant frustrations. Rats ate a batch of his peanut seeds; his first colony of rabbits mysteriously died; a worker cutting grass mistakenly chopped down all of his young mango trees; new rice varieties ordered for two years never arrived. But he continually relied on the Lord's help, and it was always there. By the time Dale returned home in November of 1978, his seeds were being enthusiastically shared by other villages, and backyard gardens were beginning to produce meals with variety as well as vitamins!

Not all our volunteers have years of specialized training. Cindy Miller, a Presbyterian from Cleveland, Ohio, spent two years in Zaire at her own expense, immediately following her graduation from high school. Cindy worked cheerfully in a dozen capacities, from house painting to barbering to planting gardens to teaching local women how to make soap. She formed a singing group with Larry Stoner, our Mennonite builder from Pennsylvania, and Joe Kirk, a Quaker from Ohio, and they were much in demand among churches in the Mbandaka area. Cindy's very presence, and her competence in responsible jobs, provided a morale boost to the Zairois women, who have little social status. And her wholehearted participation in the life of the community earned her the affection and respect of Americans and Africans alike.

Many people who have volunteered their services to Habitat have worked in building projects here in the United States rather than overseas. And some, who may not have aspirations in the home-construction field, have rendered invaluable assistance in the Habitat office in Americus. Handling the enormous volume of mail which continually moves in and out of our office may not sound as fascinating as building houses in far-off Africa or elsewhere, but the Habitat newsletters, mailings, and day-to-day communications are absolutely essential in keeping the whole effort going. And the vibrant Christian spirit that is characteristic of Habitat people makes them a joy to work with, whatever the location.

We encourage volunteers simply to offer whatever skills they have. When they do, the Lord will provide a way for these skills to be used.

Harry Sangree, a newly graduated Dartmouth engineer from Massachusetts, went to Zaire in the spring of 1979, wanting to be useful but not quite sure how. After several weeks spent in Mbandaka in culture adjustment and carpentry work, Harry found his niche. He designed an improved drainage system for the housing project there, to prevent flooding during the rainy season.

For the next three months, Harry and his Zairois helpers hand-shoveled through mud and swamp and eight-foot-high dirt piles. They cut tall grasses and trees and grubbed out stumps; they dislocated termites and black ants and water snakes. They constructed a whole network of canals. In the process, they also built three concrete bridges, each one different, in order to determine the most effective and economical design for the future. The week before Harry returned home to begin graduate school, there were four days of heavy rainstorms which inundated the project, but after a few hours of rapid runoff, the ground was already starting to dry. The next day, to Harry's immense satisfaction, the puddles were nearly gone.

The living conditions of hundreds of people have been changed and improved through the talents of this hardworking Habitat volunteer. Furthermore, as he will be the first to tell you, Harry himself will never be the same again either.

Donna Stevens, a Methodist from Angola, Indiana (you met her in chapter 1, en route with us to the celebration in Ntondo), manages at sixty to outwork most people half her age. In 1979 she spent a volunteer year in Americus doing all sorts of helpful jobs. She organized a much-needed visitor center at the Habitat office. Now we have an information headquarters for everyone who stops here—some to stay a few hours, others possibly for weeks. Donna also designed a kit containing a model Habitat house, which we send to churches and other groups as a fund-raising tool. She carefully compiled huge scrapbooks of Habitat press clippings that had accumulated from all over the world. Then she thought of Habitat T-shirts, and soon volunteers and supporters were buying them by the dozens. She paid her own way to visit Habitat projects here and overseas, and now she gives slide programs back in Indiana, making new Habitat friends wherever she goes.

Donna is another of our capable volunteers who simply placed her talents in the Lord's hands. He surely put them to good use.

Habitat's entire program rests on the shoulders of volunteers. The dedicated Christians on our boards, the work crews that travel to project sites for a week or two, the fund-raisers in local churches—all these serve without pay. (That's not to say without *reward;* these folks are certainly laying up treasures in heaven.) However, when individuals decide to volunteer longer periods of time to work on a specific project, living expenses are usually provided by their home church or denomination, or sometimes by a combination of agencies.

Volunteers come to us from all sorts of backgrounds. They are united simply by their faith and by a desire to serve God in a tangible way. Roger Miller had been on the staff of a large inner-city church in Detroit; Bruce McCrae, of Indianapolis, worked for Habitat between college (Yale) and law school. Steve Salva, from Mt. Vernon, Ohio, had been an architect; Peter Kratzat was a student from Wakarusa, Indiana; and Ron Prior, from Huntingburg, Indiana, had been in the concrete and construction business. Howard Caskey worked in the administration of a retirement home in Newton, New Jersey; his wife Jan was an artist. With the exception of the Caskeys, who went to Mbandaka for one summer, all of these volunteers contributed at least two years on overseas projects. Some are still on the job as this book is written.

If a prospective volunteer writes to us about opportunities for service, we respond by sending an application form and a set of guidelines. A visit to Americus is encouraged prior to any commitment on either side. It is important that the philosophy of Habitat be thoroughly understood, as well as the individual's personal goals and expectations.

No amount of careful orientation, however, can prepare a volunteer for all the contingencies that will have to be faced, particularly overseas. Few Americans have been exposed to poverty of the sort that they will meet in Zaire, or Guatemala, or other developing nations. But we try very hard to open the minds of prospective Habitat workers to all sorts of unexpected situations, at the same time emphasizing that, no matter what problems they encounter, the Lord is near to all who call upon Him.

Letters and reports from Habitat volunteers testify to the life-changing experiences they undergo. In 1978 Southern Baptists Dana and Sally Rominger, of Banner Elk, North Carolina, raised enough money through their home church to build a house in Zaire. Then the church, Mt. Calvary Baptist, went on to raise enough additional money so that Dana himself could go to the village of Ntondo and help build that house.

Reactions ranging from joy to deep discouragement were recorded by Dana in the diary of his two months in Africa. Because his experiences are shared, to some degree, by all our volunteers, I asked Dana's permission to include here some excerpts from his journal.

> <u>Thursday, November 30, 1978</u>
> The hard part was saying goodbye. I am on the plane to Brussels and am ready to order supper, but the menu is in French. At the top is "Poisson de l'Atlantique." I hope "poisson" means fish. Many things await me in Zaire, but I have a real sense of purpose and I know that God is with me.
>
> <u>Friday, December 1</u>
> I met Sam Mompongo in Brussels this morning, and he will be going all the way to Ntondo with me. He is director of the Habitat project there and is returning from a six-week speaking tour in the United States. We arrived in Kinshasa, the capital, at 9 P.M. Immediately the police tried to arrest us on some imaginary charges. They wanted a bribe, but we refused and they detained us about half an hour.
>
> <u>Saturday, December 2—Kinshasa</u>
> I am sharing a very small room with a Zairois man who does not speak English. I went to the market, and it is certainly different from the supermarket at home.

There is little to choose from and everything is so high, especially if it is imported. The currency here is called zaires, and one zaire is worth about one dollar at the official rate of exchange. Some typical prices: 36Z for a box of cookies; 6Z for a pound of hamburger; 100Z for a piece of cloth. The average income is 45Z a month, and most families need about 160Z worth of bread alone for a month. The only ones who can afford many of these things are the ones who are able to trade currency on the black market, in which the rate is three or four zaires for one dollar. Transportation is very hard to get also. When a bus stops there is much pushing, and people climb up the sides to crawl in the windows. If a child gets sick, the place to go is to the man on the sidewalk who has a small stand set up with several kinds of pills, which he has stolen. He does not know what he is selling and the people do not know what they are taking. Most Americans have never seen such poverty.

Monday, December 4—Mbandaka

Today Sam and I flew up the Zaire River to Mbandaka. Transportation here is very unreliable, and we got our flight just by chance. I met Dale Long, who has been up from Ntondo for a week and a half trying to get a flight to Kinshasa. He finally gave up and is going to take the riverboat Thursday. He told me that everything is scarce in Ntondo, including food, so I hope to do some shopping here.

Wednesday, December 6—Ntondo

We did our shopping this morning and I bought about 225Z worth of supplies, with 75Z of it going for half a sack of flour. I saw some sights in the marketplace that were just too pitiful to describe here. I could not keep from thinking, "Doesn't the world know what is happening here?" We started to Ntondo with the driver and five of Sam's cousins in the land rover. Every few minutes Sam would look at the driver and say *"Malembe!"* After a while Sam said to me, "The driver cannot see well. I have to tell him when we are coming to a hole in the road." It was 90 miles of rough road which took almost four hours to traverse. As we sat and talked with the volunteers after supper, a three-inch spider started crawling up the wall. I am going to bed now, but I think I will sleep with one eye open.

Thursday, December 7

I have half of a house to myself but not much furniture. I have a bamboo bed, a few wooden chairs, a table, a dresser, and a small kerosene stove. We have no electricity. The water will run out of the bathroom but not in, and we have to take baths in the lake.

Saturday, December 9

This morning we transported blocks, two at a time by hand. The time has come to admit that I am very homesick and even decided at one time to go back home. I have had to ask God many times for strength.

Sunday, December 10

I woke up this morning feeling miserable, so I went to Sam's house and told him I was ready to go home. He took me inside and we had a long talk. He told me about similar experiences he had when he was in school in America. I came away with a renewed spirit and a resolve to stay until the house is finished. I know that God is with me and He will not leave me alone. During church services I had to make a short talk with Sam translating for me. After church I had dinner with Sam's family and experienced my first real Zairois food. Just let me say that it will take me a while to get used to it.

Wednesday, December 13

I finally started work on the house. The foundation had already been dug before I came to Ntondo, so today we laid foundation blocks. I worked as a boy mason, which is a mason's helper. We have a crew of eight and none of them speaks English. They had a hard time telling me what needs to be done, but they are very patient, and when they do get through to me, it pleases them a lot. This is the friendliest group of people I have ever seen. I have been treated with kindness everywhere. Sometimes it is hard to understand how they can be so cheerful in the face of this poverty. I think it is a tribute to their Christian love. The housing here is very poor, and as I walk around the village I sometimes see a small child with a bloated, worm-filled stomach. That is a sight that hurts.

Thursday, December 14

The man who is to receive the house is in the hospital for a hernia operation. His name is Nkanga Mpolo, and he is a retired mechanic for the mission. His wife's name is Koko Londo. They have two daughters and ten grandchildren living with them.

Friday, December 15

Today the crew laid 319 blocks. I was encouraged by that. Almost everything is done by hand here. The blocks are made one at a time. When we want water to mix cement, it is almost a one-fourth mile round trip walk with a bucket. We have to climb down a steep sixty-foot bank to the lake, dip the water out, and climb back up the bank. Several trips a day are required.

Sunday, December 17

Today Sam had a small live crocodile in his kitchen. He told me that we are going to eat it tomorrow. I have had several things here that I never thought I would be eating, such as porcupine and monkey meat, and some other things that I was afraid to ask about. The thought of eating monkey meat did not bother me, but then I looked into the bowl and saw the monkey's foot in there with its claws curled up. Sometimes I ask myself what I am doing here when I could be home with Sally, living a life of ease. All I have to do to dispel that feeling is to go inside Nkanga Mpolo's present house. It was built by crisscrossing some sticks and packing mud between them. It has a palm leaf roof and no windows. When I walk inside, my eyes have to adjust to the dark, and then the only furniture I see are some bamboo beds on a dirt floor. When I step into that house, I immediately remember my purpose for being here.

Thursday, December 21

I went with Chris Lepp, the Mennonite volunteer from Canada, about 20 miles in the truck to get lumber. They had already sold it to someone else. We managed to get a few pieces of scrap lumber. Along the road we saw a lot of children walking to school. Some of the children from out-lying villages have to walk as much as ten miles a day to school. As far as I know, Sam is the only individual in this area who owns a car. He has a small car which his cousin in Kinshasa gave him, but it does not run.

Friday, December 22

Half of the crew was sick today, including me. I have had a cold for several days, but last night it got worse, so I did not work very hard. I am beginning to learn to exercise more patience with the people here. Watching them work, it is easy to let the world "lazy" come to mind, but I realize that because of the diet they live on they cannot be expected to work as hard as other people. When I consider this, I am ashamed for the times I have become impatient.

Saturday, December 23

We are off from work today through Monday for Christmas. We bought a cow to eat and divide among the workers as a bonus, so this afternoon the butchering took place behind Chris and Dodie Lepp's house. I did not take part, as I am still feeling bad. A group of volunteers came down from Mbandaka in a pickup truck the project there has gotten. They brought a lot of mail but none for me. We are so remote here that we hardly hear any news. I sometimes wonder what important events are taking place in the world that I have no way of knowing about.

Monday, December 25

Christmas. An easy time to be homesick. Whenever I heard a carol the feeling would get strong. Many times I would look at my watch and think about the things that were taking place at home. The volunteers took a sound thrashing from the home town boys in volleyball today. They were serving the ball between their legs, hitting it across the net with their heads, and just generally making us look bad.

Friday, December 29

The block work is nearing completion now. I found out that Ntondo has its own race relations problem. There are two small villages of Pygmies on the outskirts of Ntondo. They still hunt with bows and arrows and are a little more primitive than other people here, so they are considered a lower class of people. However, there is a program under way now to bring them up to an equal standard. This was started by the local people.

Monday, January 1, 1979

Tonight there was a get-together of the executive committee of the project and I was invited to attend. There was tea and cake so I went; cakes are very rare out here. The talk was of general things, and eventually Sam got around to telling about some of the things he saw on his trip. There are several local people on the committee, and as Sam explained the sensation of being cold and the sight of snow, they sat there in amazement. Finally Pastor Ngando said, "Are there people in Europe and America who do not believe in God?" Sam said, "Yes, there are many." Pastor Ngando asked, "How can that be? When people see such amazing things like snow falling, how can there be even one person who does not believe in God?" I thought that was a very good question.

Tuesday, January 2

We spent the day carrying blocks out from the school, so we did not work any on the house. One of the project workers' children died today, and another of his children died last Saturday. That makes either three or four that he has lost in a year and a half. That is a very common thing here, because the children are so undernourished that any small disease can kill them. One out of every four children here never makes it to five years of age.

Saturday, January 6

It rained part of the morning, so we did not do any masonry work, but after it stopped raining we started putting the supports for the roof together. Then the truck brought the frames for the doors and windows and we put most of those in. Chris has malaria now. The mosquitoes are really getting bad.

Tuesday, January 9

There is always a lot of excitement whenever a vehicle enters or leaves Ntondo, which is about once a week. Sam returned in the land rover from Mbandaka tonight after being there three days buying food. He brought the mail and I got my first letters. I guess I was about the happiest person in Africa.

Wednesday, January 10

The people here have found out that I am leaving soon, and I have been besieged with requests for my personal belongings. My shoes are already promised to someone, and a lot of people want my shirts, pants, and watch. One fellow offered to pay me for my watch, and I explained that I will be needing it. The next day he came up to me and said he wanted to buy my eyeglasses! Finally someone got around to asking for my underwear.

Saturday, January 13

I did not write yesterday because I have been miserably sick. I think my stomach has finally rebelled against the diet that has been forced upon it. While I was sick the carpenters put the tin on the roof. Yesterday afternoon a boat came in with 1,400 sacks of cement and 1,000 sheets of tin. Yesterday and this morning it was unloaded. My illness got me out of that backbreaking work, but it was hard to be thankful for it at the time.

Tuesday, January 16

I have now gone from a mason's helper to a carpenter's helper to a painter. I painted all day while some of the windows and doors were put in. This afternoon I met with some of the Christian men of the village, and they brought me many gifts of food. The food shortage is becoming worse, and it was hard for me to accept food from the villagers, but to have refused would have been considered very bad manners.

Friday, January 19

There was a lot of give and take today. I gave away most of my clothes, and Pastor Ngando and I passed out my canned food among the poor. Nkanga Mpolo has been periodically giving me eggs and pineapples, and today he gave me a rooster, which I in turn gave to one of the other volunteers. Again I felt ill at ease in taking it, but in a way it would have been more selfish not to have accepted. Even the poor should be able to experience the joy of giving.

Saturday, January 20

This morning was a busy time, getting ready to leave and saying goodbyes. Nkanga gave me another chicken. When we left he was standing near the edge of the village to wave at me. He will soon be moving into his new home.

Monday, January 22—Mbandaka

The morning was spent trying to get my visa extended. I thought that I had a three-month visa, but upon my arrival in Zaire we discovered it was only for

> one month. I have to have it in order to leave the country. It is ironic that I cannot leave the country until I get permission to stay.
>
> Tuesday, January 23
>
> We tried for the extension again today and were told at the immigration office that they will do it tomorrow. Whether they will or not is a matter of speculation. We went to the post office and found out that the mail has been sitting on a boat at the dock for a week. The post office does not have a car to go get it, and they said no one will lend them one. We have the pickup but very little gas, so we have to plan our trips carefully.
>
> Wednesday, January 24
>
> We went to the immigration office again this morning, and this time the head man told us that I did not have to have the visa extension. I hope he is right. I caught the flight to Kinshasa tonight. Everything went very smoothly at the airport, which is highly unusual for in-country flights.
>
> Thursday, January 25—Kinshasa
>
> There was no problem with the visa extension, and I am now on the plane in Kinshasa, waiting to take off for Brussels. The past eight weeks have been perhaps the toughest but most rewarding period of my life. There is no doubt that God has been with me and has led me every step of the way.

God continues to lead Dana Rominger. Since his return, Dana has often spoken about his experiences to churches and other organizations in his area.

"Until this mission project," he told me, "I had never been brave enough to address the church as a group, but the second Sunday after my return I had the whole morning service, and I talked twenty or thirty minutes longer than the preacher ever does. Sally commented that six months ago our pastor couldn't get me to say three words—and now he can't get me to sit down!"

Whenever you give, you receive. Habitat volunteers make enormous contributions of energy, enthusiasm, and ability along with their material resources. At the same time, they themselves are tremendously enriched. They acquire new relationships and expanded horizons and, above all, a deeper faith in God.

The First Letter of John admonishes us: "Our love should not be just words and talk; it must be true love, which shows itself in action."[1]

Habitat volunteers *are* love in action.

---

1. 1 John 3:18.

14
God's Coincidences

People are always asking me questions like "How does Habitat for Humanity grow? How do new projects get started? Where does all your support come from?"

I try to explain that the answer to every one of these questions is really simple. So simple, in fact, that most of the people in the world, some of them faithful churchgoers, continue to reject it. They are unable to accept the important promise that is basic to both the Old and the New Testaments. If we will only trust God completely, always seeking the guidance of His Holy Spirit, He will faithfully provide whatever we need, and He will bless our efforts in the most astonishing ways.

I remember a story Clarence Jordan used to tell with great relish about a newspaper reporter who appeared at Koinonia one day. He wanted to know who supported this small community.

"The Lord does," Clarence informed him.

"The Lord?" The reporter was puzzled. "No, Mr. Jordan." He tried again. "I want to know who *really* supports this place."

Clarence said he just smiled at the man and repeated, "The Lord *really* supports it."

"Mr. Jordan," the reporter rejoined, "you don't understand what I mean. I want to know who supports Koinonia. You know, how do you get your money?"

"The Lord provides it," Clarence insisted.

"Mr. Jordan, let me ask my question another way. How do you pay your bills?"

Clarence responded without hesitation, "By check."

The poor reporter was exasperated: "Mr. Jordan, you just don't seem to understand what I mean!"

"Yes, I do," Clarence replied patiently. "The problem is that *you* don't understand what *I* mean!"

As usual, Clarence's pentrating mind had gone right to the heart of the matter. The secular world demands an explanation for everything, looking in unbelief at God's constant blessings and calling them "coincidences." Habitat for Humanity people, who do believe, have learned to anticipate a lot of beautiful "coincidences." A number of these I've already told you about; I want to share some others here.

Shortly before we left Zaire in 1976, I went to the little Mbandaka airport one day to meet someone who never arrived—a not uncommon occurrence in Africa. However, three men did get off the plane, and it was obvious from their lost look that the party who was expected to meet them was not there.

"May I help you?" I inquired in French. "Do you need a ride into town?"

One of the men responded, "Yes, we were to be met by Pastor Boyaka, but he doesn't seem to be here."

"No, he isn't," I assured them. "I work for the Protestant church here, and I know Pastor Boyaka quite well. I'll take you to his office."

We all piled into my little Volkswagen and headed toward town. On the way I learned that the men were German Lutheran pastors, and that they were visiting the country on behalf of Zaire Mission, a Christian agency in Germany that rendered specialized assistance to missionary endeavors in

Zaire. As they told me of their work and I described my own, we sensed a mutual kinship. I knew Linda would like to know them as well, so I took them to Pastor Boyaka's office and made arrangements for their lodging, and then invited them to have supper at our house.

Later that evening, after a lengthy discussion of the situation in Zaire and our respective mission projects, the conversation turned to World War II. I was interested in learning something about the war from the German side. I started with Pastor Johannes Bruckemann.

"Where were you during the war?" I asked.

"Oh," he grinned, "I spent most of it in the United States. I was captured right at the beginning of the war and was taken to the U.S. as a prisoner."

"Is that so?" I queried. "Where did they take you?"

"Alabama."

"Alabama?" I was surprised. "That's my home state. Where in Alabama were you?"

"Opelika."

"Opelika?" I was amazed. "Why, that's just a few kilometers from my father's place at Lanett, Alabama! Not more than a thirty-minute drive away! What did you do in Opelika?"

"I was on a pulpwood crew. We cut pine trees in the forests near Opelika."

I couldn't believe my ears.

"You cut pulpwood in the woods around Opelika? Where?"

As he described the road they took out of Opelika to get to the areas where they were cutting, I realized that he had been on the crew cutting trees on that farm my dad had bought on the Lanett-Lafayette highway.

"Why, Pastor Bruckemann," I exclaimed, "you were cutting trees on my daddy's farm!"

What a fantastic "coincidence." We were sitting in the middle of Africa, and I had just met a German prisoner of war that I had probably seen, and perhaps even talked to, some thirty years before in the pine woods of East Alabama! (When my daddy was negotiating to buy that farm off the Lafayette highway, I would go with him into the woods where the

German prisoners were. I would mingle with them and try to carry on a conversation, though most did not know any English.)

By the time the evening was over, our friendship was fast and firm. The pastors wanted us to visit them in Germany on our way back to the United States, and addresses and phone numbers were exchanged as we parted.

Our whole family did visit Pastor Bruckemann and his wife in July 1976, on our trip home. We also spent a day with Pastor Kurt Bonk and his wife, another of the travelers I just "happened" to encounter at the Mbandaka airport.

A few months later, when *Bokotola* was published, describing our experience in Zaire, I sent both of them copies. Pastor Bruckemann responded with one of the most beautiful letters I have ever received. He told us the book had been a great joy to him, especially since he did not have a good house when he was growing up, and he knew how much a decent home meant to a family. He said he wept frequently as he read about our efforts to provide homes for the poor through the ministry of Habitat for Humanity. He concluded the letter by saying that he was determined to get the book printed in German so that Christians in his country could read it; in the meantime he ordered a supply of copies in English and began circulating them.

With Pastor Bonk's help, he succeeded in having *Bokotola* translated into German, and the first edition was published in December 1978. As a result, German Christians wanted to contribute to the work of Habitat, so Pastor Bonk set up an account with the United Evangelical Mission in Wuppertal for that purpose. Later, he arranged for me a week of speaking engagements in Germany during May 1980. This exciting trip included addressing a World Mission Conference in Essen with 3,000 people in attendance. Interest in Habitat's ministry continues to build in Europe; and it began with a "chance" meeting at a tiny airport in Zaire.

God has arranged coincidences which have brought us some wonderful Habitat volunteers. One of these was Jeff Buttram, of Mantua, New Jersey.

At twenty-three, Jeff had had a year and a half of study at

Rutgers University; then he had dropped out for a succession of jobs, including one in housing construction. In the fall of 1977, Jeff was attending classes at Glassboro College, near his home, and still wondering what direction he should take with his life. It was time to choose his courses for the spring semester, but he just couldn't make up his mind.

Jeff turned his decision over to the Lord.

"I asked Him to let me know exactly what He had planned for me," Jeff told me later, "and I reminded Him that I needed an answer in less than two weeks!"

That Sunday, Jeff attended the Mantua United Methodist Church. On the way out, the pastor stopped him.

"Jeff," he asked, "how'd you like to go to Zaire? I just got some information about a housing project there, and our denomination will provide support for a volunteer builder."

At that point, Jeff didn't even know where Zaire was. But he recognized one of God's coincidences when he saw one. Within six weeks he arrived in Americus for orientation with our office and with the building project there. His passport and visa were processed in record time, and in January 1978 Jeff went to Ntondo to work for a period of fifteen months under the sponsorship of the United Methodists.

Now back in the States, Jeff is pursuing an engineering degree with new enthusiasm. He goes out speaking and showing his slides of Africa wherever he finds an audience, and the message of Habitat continues to spread.

In the spring of 1978, while Jeff was still in Ntondo, we had a call from Pat Clark, an outstanding young black woman from Salem, New Jersey. Pat, a Baptist, was a longtime friend of Diane Scott and her family, also of Salem. (Diane had done the editorial work on *Bokotola,* and was at that point writing *Habitat Happenings,* our monthly newsletter.) Pat (then a junior at Smith College in Massachusetts) told us that she had just finished reading *Bokotola* twice, and that she wanted to spend her summer working on a Habitat project in Zaire. Pat herself could not underwrite this—she was attending college on a full scholarship and working forty hours a week at McDonald's besides. So, back in New Jersey, Diane began fund raising among Pat's friends and local church groups.

A travel agent had told Pat that her round trip expenses would be $1,566. Money began to come in; the smallest gift was 75¢, and the largest was $300. By the first week in June, when she left for her three months of work, the Pat Clark Fund amounted to exactly $1567.05.

When we paid for the ticket, however, it turned out that there was an additional unanticipated charge of $5. Well, we thought, the Lord knew we needed the extra money even though we didn't know it, and it is probably on its way. The next day we received an unsolicited check for $5 toward Pat's expenses from Rosa Page Welch, a Habitat board member from Denver, Colorado. And then the money stopped coming.

The Lord always knows what we need, and when. In learning to trust Him, we also learn that Jesus' promise, "Ask, and ye shall receive," is entirely true.

As I write this, Pat Clark is back in Zaire. She was so affected by her experience there that she decided to return for two years between her college graduation and her entrance into law school. Once again Diane has been fund raising, and once again Pat's support has been coming in steadily from interested friends and churches, including Dexter Avenue King Memorial Baptist Church in Montgomery, Alabama, former pastorate of Dr. Martin Luther King, Jr. (and current pastorate of Dr. G. Murray Branch, a Habitat board member). We don't yet know where all the money will come from, but what we do know is that there will be enough.

Habitat's base of support is thoroughly ecumenical, and we are always glad for opportunities to broaden that base.

In August of 1979 I was invited to give two lectures at the summer program at Chautauqua, New York. Dr. Ralph Loew, director of the Department of Religion there, is the distinguished pastor emeritus of Holy Trinity Lutheran Church in Buffalo, New York.

Dr. Loew had already become vitally interested in Habitat as one of the "new forms of mission"—which happened to be the topic of their study for that week. After I had spent several days with him at Chautauqua, I told Dr. Loew that we had not had active Lutheran participation in our ministry up to that point, and I invited him to serve on our Board of Advisors. He readily agreed to do this.

When I boarded the plane in Buffalo to return to Georgia, I found myself sitting next to a husband and wife who just happened to be longtime members of Dr. Loew's church. Never one to miss an opportunity, I began telling these new Lutheran friends about Habitat. Later, I sent them a copy of *Bokotola,* and they have been faithful contributors ever since.

Shortly after I arrived home from Chautauqua, Ralph and Jane Gnann, of Plains, Georgia, came to see me about volunteering for work in Zaire. Ralph has had all sorts of mechanical and construction experience, and Jane is trained both as a teacher and as a practical nurse. A few months later the Gnanns were accorded full support for a three-year term in Zaire by their denomination—the Lutheran Church in America. As this book goes to press, Ralph and Jane and their two children are studying French in southern France, on their way to the building project in Ntondo.

While we were in conversation with the Gnanns about possibilities for work with Habitat, I received an unexpected invitation to speak at the All Saints Lutheran Church in Kansas City, Kansas. This was my first opportunity to address a Lutheran group since returning from Africa, and as a result, a number of new supporters were added to our mailing list.

Through a variety of other happenings too complicated to detail, still more members of this denomination became involved in Habitat during the latter half of 1979. One surprising occurrence followed another. Finally, we stopped being surprised and began simply to accept each new incident as a further example of "the Lutheran coincidences." And we gave thanks that another large and active group of Christians had joined us in this great venture.

Then there was the day in the spring of 1979 when I was talking on the phone with Geoff Van Loucks in California.

Geoff's Almaden Valley United Church of Christ in San José is pastored by a small dynamo of a man named Jack Takayanagi. Jack had so fired up his congregation about Habitat that they had already purchased 1,000 copies of *Bokotola;* they were raising house-building funds with paper drives, aluminum can collections, a cookbook, and sales of Koinonia peanuts; and they had set up a speakers' bureau, calling themselves "Habitat, West," to tell the story to other groups in California. Geoff was president of this effort. He had called our office to order more brochures and promotional material.

I began telling Geoff about the sentimental journey Linda and I were planning in July. We were returning to visit the projects in Zaire we had left three years before and to participate in the big dedication service in the village of Ntondo.

Suddenly I had an idea.

"Geoff, why don't you come along? You've been so involved with what's happening there through your fund raising. This would give you a chance to learn what Habitat is really all about. We are going to be gone from June 29 to July 18. How about it?"

"Come on, Millard!" was the reply. "I'd love to, you know that—but you, of all people, also know what a trial attorney's schedule is like. There is just no way I can take off from here for that long—." His voice trailed off.

"Well, we'd sure like to have you with us. Think about it. You'd have to realize, though, that if you did go, it would certainly change your life."

We chatted another minute or two and then hung up.

The next day Geoff called back.

"Millard, you won't believe this. I'm going!" He was ecstatic. "After I talked to you yesterday, just out of curiosity I checked my calendar. I was absolutely amazed. It's crammed with stuff right up to June 29, and again after July 18. But there's *nothing* in between! No hearings, no trials—not even a dental appointment! I went home and discussed the trip with Dolores—and you know that she's been working as hard for Habitat as I have—and she said I should go. So it's settled. I'm going!"

Geoff did go, thanks to another of God's coincidences. We had an exciting trip (you read about it back in chapter 1), and the experience turned an already staunch supporter of Habitat into a super-supporter. And at least once a week we get more news at the Habitat office about the enlarging activities of the enthusiastic committee at Habitat, West in San José, California.

A Presbyterian businessman in Kansas City, Missouri, set in motion a whole string of God's coincidences, beginning in 1977. John Pritchard, who had thirty years' experience in the construction and marketing of precut homes, had been asking God for some time to indicate what new directions He might have for his life. Knowing his interest in housing, John's pastor gave him a copy of *Bokotola.* As soon as John had read the book, he got in touch with us, and it just "happened" that I would be in Kansas City within a couple of weeks.

By the time I had talked with John in his hometown, and he and his wife Mary had made a subsequent visit to the Habitat office in Georgia, he was convinced that here was a task to which he had been led by the Holy Spirit. He took steps to free himself from the day-to-day operation of his business, and he and Mary began to work virtually full-time for Habitat.

Initially they decided to seek out people who were knowledgeable about their city and who might be willing to help form a Kansas City Habitat committee. Apparently the Holy Spirit had been moving in some other lives as well. Every person John approached—most of them people he had never met before—accepted his challenge without hesitation. Within three weeks the Pritchards had assembled a working committee of eight.

The first time the group met together, they discovered that their membership was equally divided between whites and blacks, and that within this rather randomly selected gathering there were represented eight different skills or professions: ministry, homemaking, law, insurance, architecture, construction, social work, and administration. They had every kind of expertise that would be needed to launch a Habitat project!

Their next step was to try to obtain land in Kansas City. The committee settled upon a four-square-block area in a neighborhood that seemed fairly stable, but in which there were a number of vacant lots, the result of city demolition of substandard housing.

John was assigned the responsibility of paying a visit to a man in an outlying suburb who owned a large corner lot in the target area. The committee hoped to be able to purchase this plot at a reasonable price as their first investment and then to obtain through the city other nearby parcels which had been foreclosed for taxes.

Some time later, John described the interview to me.

"I was really apprehensive about this meeting," he said, "and on the way in I stopped and asked the Lord for help. The man who owned this ground was a judge. He listened to me so soberly I might have been on trial. And the longer I talked, the sillier I felt. Here I was, trying to persuade this imposing gentleman that a group of idealistic visionaries with almost no money would be able to build a lot of homes for poor families in the inner city. Standing before his desk, I felt like a schoolboy facing the principal—me, a gray-haired sixty-three! I honestly expected at any moment to be laughed out of the office.

"But he continued to listen thoughtfully, and he appeared quite willing to hear me out. When I had finished, there was a moment of silence. He studied me intently.

"Finally he responded.

" 'Mr. Pritchard,' he said, 'it's interesting that you should raise this question. For some time I have been considering the possibility of donating that property to some charitable organization and taking the corresponding tax deduction.' "

Wow!

"As I drove the fifty miles back to Kansas City," John told me, "I was dumbfounded, jubilant, disbelieving, and believing—all at the same time!"

When the Habitat boards held their fall meeting in October 1979, we were hosted by the Pritchards' First Presbyterian Church of Liberty, Missouri. And one of the highlights of that gathering was a groundbreaking ceremony for the first Kansas City Habitat house, on the lot donated by the judge. The committee has since acquired nine more parcels of land from the city, and their goal is to build five homes a year over the next ten years.

They'll make it.

When one of our Habitat board members, Sandy Owen, was returning to her home in Austin, Texas, from that same Kansas City board meeting, she kept thinking and praying about ways she might be able to get the Habitat message to more people. Sandy and her husband Dan had been missionaries in Zaire under the Christian Church (Disciples of Christ) when Linda and I visited there back in 1966. The Owens had shown us some of the dreadful housing in Mbandaka. Sandy told us about a mission employee who begged from them one of their steel shipping barrels. He wanted it for his brother, who had no place to sleep. Thereafter the man stored all his possessions in the barrel during the day, with a padlock on it; at night, he crawled into it and slept.

Sandy and Dan had also introduced us to the church's floundering block-and-sand project in Mbandaka, which later became such a big factor in the community-building effort. Although they returned to the States in 1971, the Owens continued to keep in touch with us. They supported our work in Zaire enthusiastically and looked for ways to widen that support.

About two weeks after the Kansas City meeting, the Owens, en route to another church conference, stopped at a fast-food place in Waco. At the next table there just happened to be sitting three Disciples staff members, on their way to a program-planning meeting. During their conversation, one of the staff people asked Sandy whether she had any suggestions for speakers for their biennial Southwest Regional Assembly in Austin in the fall of 1980. It just happened that she did.

Shortly after this encounter, I received an invitation to tell the Habitat story to a thousand Christians representing 466 churches throughout Texas and New Mexico—and my calendar just happened to be open on that date!

I could go on and on. The only response I can give to the questions about how Habitat for Humanity grows, and where our support comes from, is to recount experiences like these. Compassionate Christians, placing their trust where it belongs, decide to band together in order to reach out to their brothers and sisters in need. And one miracle follows another.

The world stares at all these happenings and foolishly calls them "coincidences." We know that they are answered prayers.

15

A Pebble in a Pond

"Linda, I sure hope you and Millard can get something going over there. It would be fantastic if volunteers like the ones here at Koinonia could work for a while on a housing project in a developing country. When they return, they could train others. And their experience would help us all become more aware of the tremendous needs overseas."

It was early 1973 at Koinonia, and Linda and I were soon to leave with our family for three years in Zaire. The speaker was Don Mosley. At that point he and his wife Carolyn and their two children had lived at Koinonia for more than a year. Don was now supervising the housing program, and our families had become close friends.

The occasion was a farewell supper at the Mosleys'. The evening had been an emotional time for us all. None of us had any idea what might be accomplished with the practically defunct block-and-sand project Linda and I had seen in Mbandaka—or with any of the church's other efforts at economic development there. But we were totally committed to the low-cost housing program that had been launched at Koinonia, and we had determined that the same experiment should be undertaken in Africa.

So we sat around the dinner table tossing ideas and hopes and dreams at each other, and not wanting to say good-bye.

Don, a mechanical engineer who had served with the Peace Corps in Korea and Malaysia before he came to Koinonia, kept returning to the same theme.

"There's so much for Americans to learn through experiencing life in the so-called Third World countries," he said. "If we could send Christian volunteers with specific skills to a housing project to live among the people, immersed in their culture and their language—but at the same time working *in partnership* with them. . . . Boy, that could make a tremendous contribution. On both sides!"

Don still kids me that he can remember the exact moment when I became really excited. His words began to explode in my head. I could hardly stay in my chair.

"Well, why not?" I burst out. "Why not have projects *all over the world?* There are *millions* of people living in slums. *Everywhere!*"

The four of us thought about that wild proposal for a minute.

"You know," I insisted, "this could be a historic moment. If this idea ever caught on, who knows where it might lead?"

Twelve months later, Don was in Zaire with us. He spent three weeks there, slogging across swampy fields, cutting through thick vegetation, and climbing giant anthills, in order to survey a strip of empty land right in the middle of the city of Mbandaka, known to the Africans as Bokotola.

The wild idea was on its way.

In the summer of 1980, as this book is being published, Habitat for Humanity programs are planned or under way in twenty-six locations in the United States and overseas. Enough land has been acquired for more than 2,000 houses, and nearly a fourth of these are already built. More inquiries are coming in all the time. Christians have heard about this new kind of ministry, and they want to know how to become involved. Some offer fund-raising or financial support; others are interested in serving as volunteers on a project. Sometimes they ask, "How can we begin a Habitat building program in our area?"

We try to answer every request and to encourage every effort. At the same time, we do not minimize the problems that will have to be faced. In the original manuscript of *Bokotola,* I included a chapter titled "Obstacles." It detailed some of the difficulties we encountered in Zaire: a preposterous bureaucracy, cultural conflicts, tropical diseases, perpetual shortages, skyrocketing inflation, thievery, ignorance, superstition. The publisher insisted that this section be removed, with parts of it dispersed through the rest of the book. Taken all at once, he said, the effect of these experiences on the reader was too hopelessly depressing!

Whenever we take time to look carefully around us at the world's terrible need, and whenever we realize the incredible obstacles we will encounter when we try to reach out to that need, it is indeed possible to feel utterly frustrated and helpless. And to give up.

But Christians have access to a source of indescribable Power which offers a solution to every problem and a way around or through or over every obstacle. Thanks to this Power, the ministry of Habitat for Humanity keeps growing.

We have never had an impressive budget or a big advertising program. Our office staff is mostly volunteers, and the administrative salaries we do have are fully underwritten by pledges from board members. Our international headquarters is located in a small remodeled home on a side street in Americus, Georgia.

What we have is a magnificent God-given idea, one which is spreading to many countries of the world. Like a small pebble dropped into a large pond, Habitat started without a big splash. But the ripples going out from it form ever-enlarging circles of concern and love.

The housing program that began at Koinonia spread to three locations in Zaire; in February 1979 a National Habitat for Humanity Committee was formed in Kinshasa to coordinate the proliferating projects. And when the town of Ntondo, in Zaire, began their building project, other towns around Lake Tumba got so caught up with the hope of improving their housing that soon eleven neighboring villages had begun raising funds and stockpiling sand, trying desperately to become a part of this venture themselves. Christian groups in other parts of Zaire (and in other African countries, particularly Uganda and Zambia) have requested assistance in launching their own Habitat projects. Church workers in poverty areas in the Carribean, in South America, and in Asia are contacting us for more information.

In North America, a strong commitment to Habitat's ministry is developing among Christians from every kind of church background you might name. There is involvement from all age groups; small children help to build houses with Bible school offerings, while retired people volunteer their skills in every job from laying blocks to stuffing envelopes. And amazing things begin to happen when just one person wholeheartedly pitches in to work.

Back in 1976 I spoke to a human relations council in St. Petersburg, Florida, about our experiences in Zaire. Following the meeting, a young man came up to talk to me.

"I'm Richard Byrd," he said. "I am really interested in the project you talked about today, and I want to help. As a college student, I don't have much cash, but I do have a couple of suggestions."

Richard's first thought was relatively simple. He had enough money to purchase a copy of *Bokotola* for every public library in St. Petersburg, and he proceeded to do this.

His second idea was incredibly ambitious. He wanted to write a letter to the editor of *every* daily newspaper in the United States and Canada about Habitat for Humanity. That would be more than 1,400 individually written letters! He was convinced that many of these would be published and that they would generate new support for the building projects.

I thanked Richard for his impressive offer, and encouraged him. But when I returned home the next day, I promptly forgot about his proposal. Many people make grand promises in moments of inspiration and just as quickly lose their enthusiasm when they return to everyday responsibilities.

But Richard wasn't like that. Soon I received a follow-up letter from him.

> Could you please send me the names and addresses of key Habitat people around the country? I would like

> to arrange with them to mail the letters to newspapers in their respective states. Editors are more likely to use material which comes from local people. I will do all the letters and address the envelopes.

We quickly complied with Richard's request, and he began feverishly writing. Many of the letters were done by hand; others he typed. As soon as he completed a batch for a particular area, he put them in a big manila envelope and sent them to a Habitat supporter in that area; postage was supplied by another helpful board member. The recipient would sign the letters and mail them out.

Over a period of many months, Richard personally completed more than 1,400 letters explaining the work of Habitat for Humanity. We do not know how many of these letters were published, but we received clippings of a great many, as well as responses from people who read them.

One of the persons who helped Richard with his project was Dan Griffin, then pastor of the First Baptist Church in Winston-Salem, North Carolina. Dan, who was already enlarging Habitat's support through his own congregation, agreed to sign and mail letters to all the daily papers in both North and South Carolina.

And one of the persons who read the letter in the *Charlotte Observer* was a young surveyor named Dana Rominger. A year later Dana was working as a Habitat volunteer in Ntondo. You read about some of his experiences in chapter 13.

When Ronn Kreps, a college student of the Christian Reformed Church from Prinsburg, Minnesota, learned that a volunteer had raised money for a house in Zaire and then gone out to build it, he asked, "Why can't I do that?"

The answer was—he could. Ronn plunged in, raised his transportation costs plus $2,000 for a house in Ntondo, and then went over and built it in the summer of 1979. The ripples from Richard Byrd's pebble are still widening, years later.

One of the most remarkable "ripple effects" that Habitat has felt began in the Plymouth Congregational Church in Plymouth, New Hampshire. The pastor, P. V. George, is a native of India, with a particular awareness of the vast world-wide need for good housing. In 1974, when Linda and I were launching the project in Mbandaka and had no idea where the money would come from, this church sent funds to build the very first house. But that was only the beginning. In the years since, the faithful supporters in this 300-member congregation have steadily increased their commitment until they have built *five* more houses—and their goal is to continue to build at least one house per year! At the same time, the regular budget of the church, and other special mission appeals as well, continue to grow annually. As P. V. says, "We have learned that the more we dare, the more we can give."

In addition, the people from Plymouth promote Habitat everywhere they go. When one member visited New York City in 1977, he introduced his friend David Rowe, pastor of the Church in the Gardens in Forest Hills, to this new ministry. David got excited about Habitat. Since then, the Forest Hills church has fulfilled a $10,000 pledge to the Kinshasa project, sold 1,500 copies of *Bokotola,* sent five volunteers to work in Americus, and provided the Habitat board with its indispensable treasurer—the Reverend David Rowe!

And the Forest Hills folks tell others about Habitat everywhere they go. And so on. . . .

As each new Habitat house is completed, the owners' payments return to the Fund, and the work expands. Although the payments are nominal, at least once a month the fortunate families, knowing that this money is being recycled to build more houses, are obligated to think about others who are in need. Furthermore, the new owners are expected to donate labor (and if possible, gifts of money as well) to help their neighbors as they have been helped. They are also encouraged to accelerate their house payments whenever they can, making possible the purchase of more blocks and mortar to build still more houses.

As each project gets under way in a new location, people hear about what Habitat is doing, and the growing involvement continues. When Linda and I were in Ntondo for their service of dedication, we visited several of the neighboring villages—all equally poor—which have formed local Habitat committees in an effort to launch their own projects. We saw great piles of sand being hand-gathered and building blocks determinedly being pressed out one at a time. In the village of Bikoro, the new committee eagerly exhibited a carefully drawn diagram for rebuilding the entire town—*700 houses.* At that moment I was really able to believe, with the Psalmist, that "the hope of the poor will not be crushed forever."[1]

The growth of this venture of faith and its impact on the lives of thousands of people, recipients and donors alike, have overwhelmed all of us who have been at the center of its blossoming. We have sought simply to carry out the command of our Lord: "Go, then, to all peoples everywhere, and make them my disciples."[2] And we have tried to make a visionary out of every life we touch, to fill every person with a zeal to do Christ's work in the world.

In his speech at the Ntondo dedication service, Sam Mompongo pointed out that "the work of Habitat proclaims the gospel of Jesus Christ by *acts.*" He went on to call Habitat for Humanity a "revolution of benevolence."

> It is a *Christian* revolution. Ntondo no longer has only Baptist missionaries and volunteers, but also Mennonite, United Church of Christ, and Methodist. We do not build only for the Protestants, but also for the Catholics; not only for the faithful of the church, but also for the pagans—an aspect incontestably revolutionary. This is the will of our Saviour, who wants us to be one.
>
> Habitat is also a *social* revolution. The penetration of foreigners into our daily lives, working with us, sharing life with us, eating our food (caterpillars, crocodiles, "monkey-burgers"!); the coming together of the Bantus and the Pygmies, living together in decent homes—the walls which have separated us are demolished, and in their place we build mutual respect.
>
> Another revolution is *economic.* Habitat has already incited the local population to launch economic activities of all kinds: woodworking, fishing, agriculture, baking. And numerous individuals have introduced requests to our committee to launch other local enterprises.

Habitat for Humanity believes that "a decent house in a decent community" is not just a catchy phrase on our letterhead. It is a basic human need. Those of us fortunate enough to have such a blessing ought to be reaching out to help those who don't, encouraging them in turn to reach out still farther.

We cannot possibly imagine how far the Lord will enlarge this revolutionary venture in the years ahead, but we are certain that the Habitat concept will succeed anywhere. There are just three essential criteria.

First, every project must have a nucleus of dedicated Christian leaders who are willing to abandon the world's standards and to substitute the audacious economics of Jesus in their dealings with His people in need. Second, the families who will occupy and own the houses must be totally involved in the building process. And third, there must always be love in the mortar joints. When all these conditions are present, the effort cannot fail.

The writer of Proverbs admonishes us to "do good to those who need it. Never tell your neighbor to wait until tomorrow if you can help him now."[3] John the Baptist is more explicit when he tells us that "whoever has two shirts must give one to the man who has none, and whoever has food must share it."[4] And Jesus makes it really personal: "Whenever you did this for one of the least important of these brothers of mine, you did it for me!"[5]

If it bothers you a little that you sleep at night on a clean pillow in a comfortable bed, while in many places around the world your neighbors toss restlessly on floors of damp earth, perhaps it's time you did something about that situation. Perhaps you would like to cast your pebble into the pond with us. Then we can rejoice together, watching our circles constantly widen, touching and strengthening and enriching more and more lives.

It may be that God is calling you to volunteer for work on a Habitat project in Zaire or Guatemala or the United States, or to launch a new one in Uganda or Zambia or Atlanta. Perhaps you should become a regular Habitat contributor and try to get your local church involved in this ministry. On the other hand, you may find yourself being called into service with your own denominational mission agency. Maybe the Lord wants you to go to seminary and prepare for the ministry. Or if you're already there, He could be suggesting that you drop out and serve Him in other ways! You may feel moved to do something about that slum in your town. Perhaps you should take in a foster child or a refugee family—or you may simply need to visit that elderly lady down the street. It could be that it is time to quit your job and move to an Indian reservation—or to stay right where you are and double your pledge to your church.

Wherever you live, you can be a faithful disciple of Christ. And whatever your resources or abilities are, God is ready to use them to work new miracles for His people in need. Like Isaiah of old, your response to the Lord's call must simply be, "Here am I; send me!"

---

1. Psalms 9:18.
2. Matthew 28:19.
3. Proverbs 3:27–28.
4. Luke 3:11.
5. Matthew 25:40.

Appendixes

Appendix A

Project Locations

Habitat for Humanity building programs are under way in the locations listed below.

SPONSORED PROJECTS (Habitat for Humanity supplies funds and personnel):

Mbandaka, Zaire
Ntondo, Zaire
Kinshasa, Zaire
Gulu, Uganda
Aguacatan, Guatemala

AFFILIATED PROJECTS (Habitat for Humanity guidelines are followed, but responsibility for generating funds and recruiting personnel rests with a local committee):

Americus, Georgia
Beaumont, Texas
Denver, Colorado
Fort Myers, Florida
Immokalee, Florida
John's Island, South Carolina
Kansas City, Missouri
Morgan and Scott counties, Tennessee
Paducah, Kentucky
San Antonio, Texas
Tucson, Arizona

For further information about the ministry of Habitat for Humanity, write or call

Habitat for Humanity, Inc.
419 West Church Street
Americus, Georgia 31709

(912) 924-6935

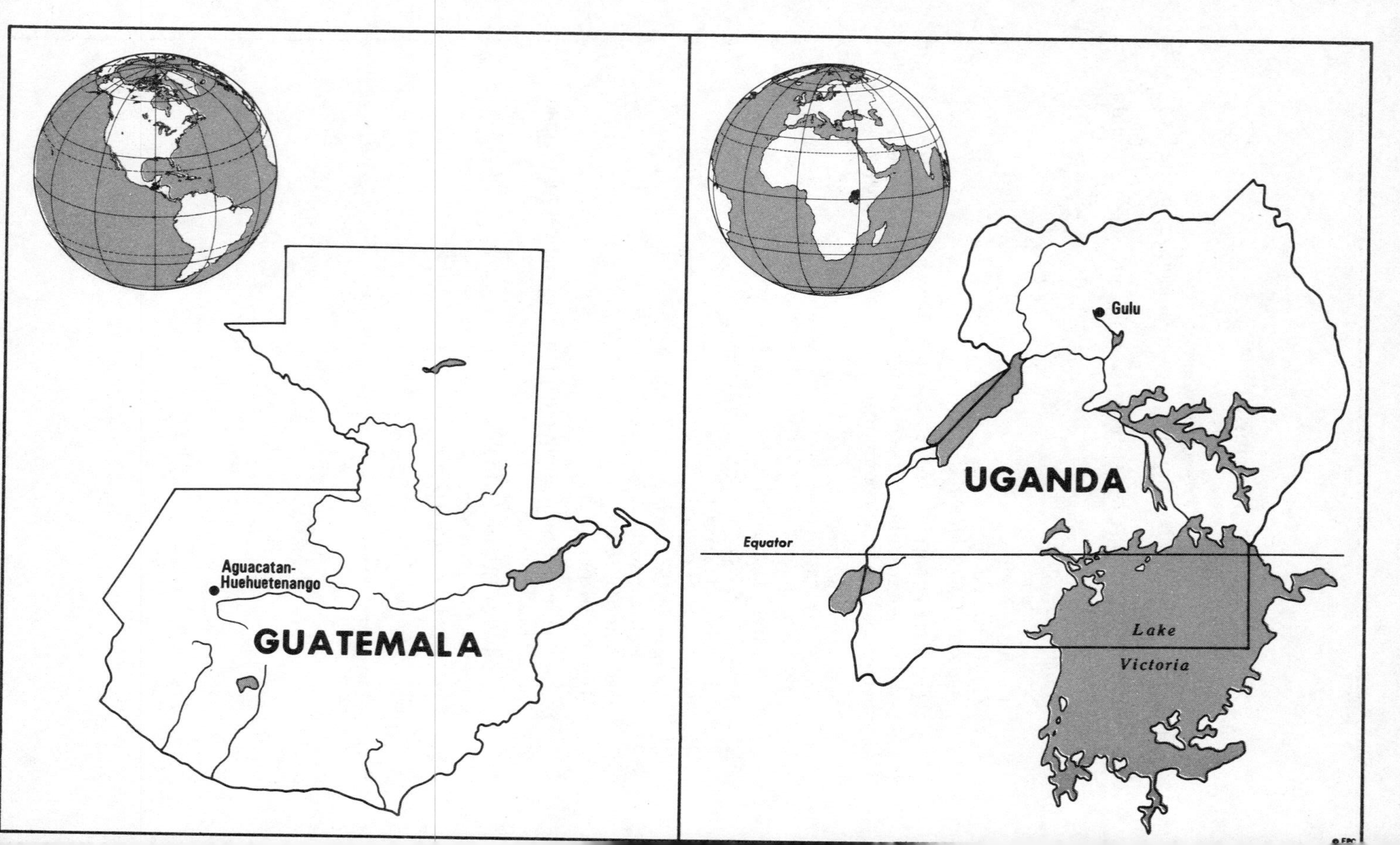

Aguacatan-
Huehuetenango
GUATEMALA
Gulu
UGANDA
Equator
Lake
Victoria

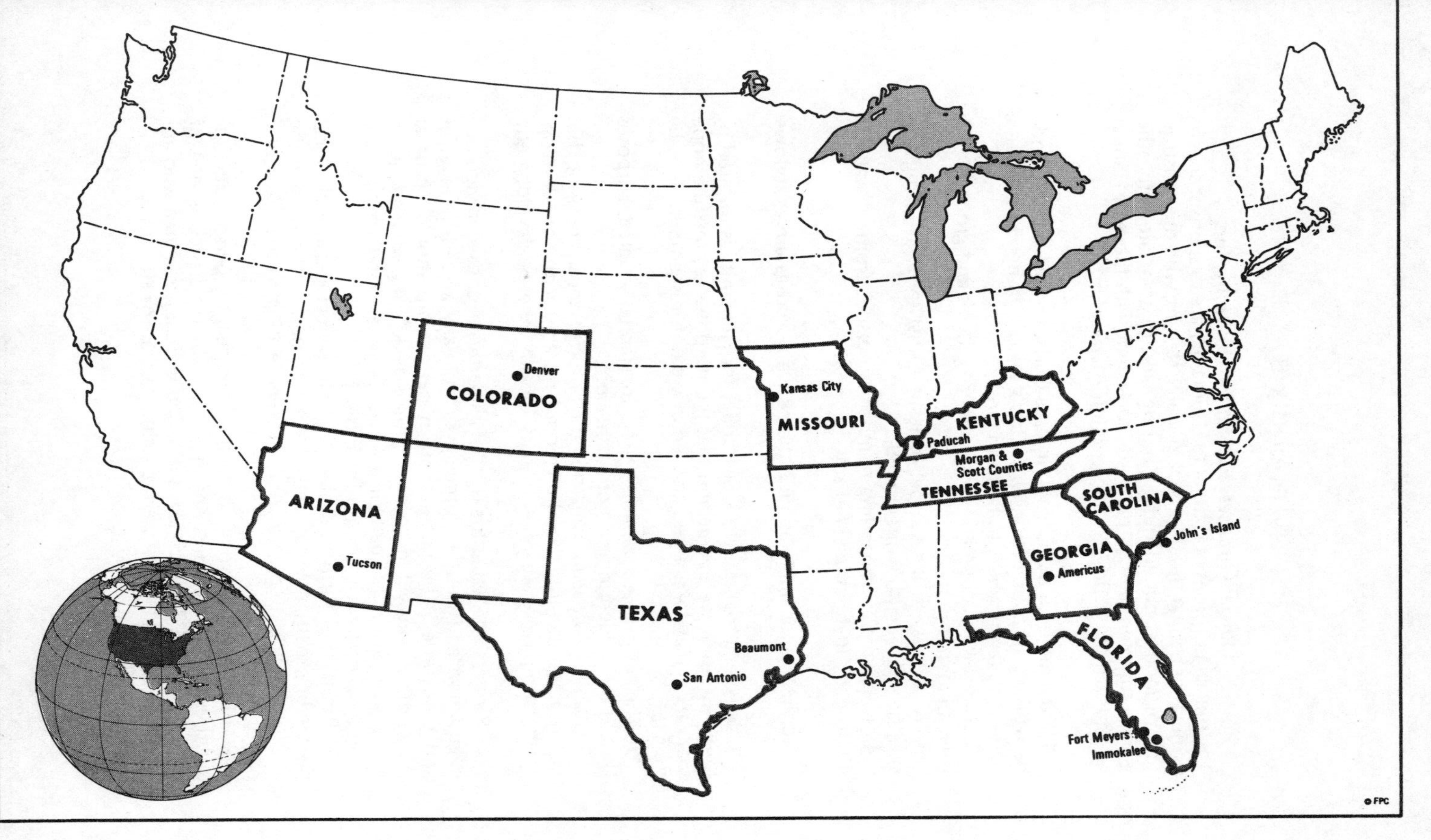
COLORADO
Denver
MISSOURI
Kansas City
KENTUCKY
Paducah
Morgan &
Scott Counties
TENNESSEE
SOUTH
CAROLINA
John's Island
GEORGIA
Americus
FLORIDA
Fort Meyers
Immokalee
ARIZONA
Tucson
TEXAS
Beaumont
San Antonio
© FPC

Appendix B

Official Purposes: Habitat for Humanity, Inc.

The official purposes of Habitat for Humanity are to sponsor specific projects in habitat development globally, starting with the construction of modest but adequate housing, and to associate with other groups functioning with purposes consistent with those of Habitat, as stated in the Articles of Incorporation, namely:

1. To witness to the Gospel of Jesus Christ throughout the world by working in cooperation with God's people in need to create a better habitat in which to live and work.

2. To work in cooperation with other agencies and groups which have a kindred purpose.

3. To witness to the Gospel of Jesus Christ through loving acts and the spoken and written word.

4. To enable an expanding number of persons from all walks of life to participate in this ministry.

Guidelines for implementing the above purposes are as follows:

1. Believing that the work of Habitat for Humanity is inspired by the Holy Spirit, we understand that the purposes express the hope that others may be grasped and led in yet unforeseen ministries by the Holy Spirit.

2. The term *in cooperation* used in Habitat's stated purposes should be defined in terms of *partnership.*

3. *Adequate housing* as used in the purposes means housing, but much more, including total environment; e.g., economic development, compassionate relationships, health, energy development, etc.

4. *Partnership* implies the right of all parties to engage in vigorous negotiation and the development of mutually agreed-upon goals and procedures. The negotiation in partnership should occur at each project and will include such items as defining what adequate housing means in that particular project, who are God's needy, and what local entity will control the project.

5. *Partnership* further implies that all project personnel—local people or expatriate volunteers—have a primary relationship to the local committee in regard to all matters relating to that particular project.

6. A primary concern in all matters is respect for persons, including their culture, visions, and dignity. Habitat's stance is one of responding to expressed needs of a people in a given area who are seeking a relationship of *partner* with Habitat for Humanity.

7. All Habitat projects must establish a Fund for Humanity, and financing of houses and other ventures must be on a noninterest basis. Each Fund for Humanity will be funded through voluntary gifts, both in cash and in kind, grants, interest-free loans, all from individuals, churches, other groups, and foundations. All repayments from houses or other Habitat-financed ventures will also be returned to the local Fund for Humanity. Finally, Habitat projects may operate enterprises which will generate funds for the local Fund for Humanity.

Appendix C

Habitat for Humanity Boards

An ecumenical Board of Directors and Board of Advisors guide the work of Habitat for Humanity. These dedicated Christians travel all over the country at their own expense to attend meetings (on four occasions Bill Clarke even journeyed to Africa for Habitat), they devote great chunks of time to fund raising and promotion, and they contribute their diverse skills in countless other ways.

Board of Directors
(April 1980)

NAME	CITY	DENOMINATION
Dr. Al Bartholomew	New York, N.Y.	United Church of Christ
*Dr. G. Murray Branch	Atlanta, Ga.	Progressive National Baptist
Dr. Harry Bredeweg	Indianapolis, Ind.	United Church of Christ
*Bill Clarke	Canton, Ohio	Presbyterian, U.S.A.
Rev. William Clemmons	Wake Forest, N.C.	Southern Baptist
*Mary Emeny	Bushland, Tex.	Ecumenical
*Sam Emerick	Port Charlotte, Fla.	United Methodist
Juan Garcia	Immokalee, Fla.	Roman Catholic
Dr. Robert Gemmer	St. Petersburg, Fla.	Church of the Brethren
Dr. Harry Haines	New York, N.Y.	United Methodist
*Dr. Grover L. Hartman	Indianapolis, Ind.	United Methodist
Rev. Robert Miller	East Cleveland, Ohio	Presbyterian, U.S.A.
Mompongo Mo Imana	Zaire, Africa	Baptist Community of Zaire River
*Don Mosley	Comer, Ga.	Ecumenical
Dr. Robert G. Nelson	Indianapolis, Ind.	Disciples
Rev. Vern Preheim	Akron, Pa.	Mennonite
John Pritchard	Liberty, Mo.	Presbyterian, U.S.A.
*Rev. David J. Rowe	Forest Hills, N.Y.	American Baptist
Rev. M. Jack Takayanagi	San José, Calif.	United Church of Christ
Geoff Van Loucks	Los Gatos, Calif.	United Church of Christ
Rosa Page Welch	Denver, Colo.	Disciples
Dennis Wikerd	Ontario, Canada	Mennonite
Bob Wood	Westport, Conn.	United Church of Christ

*Executive Committee

Board of Advisors
(April 1980)

NAME	CITY	DENOMINATION
Marian Allman	Montgomery, Ala.	Progressive National Baptist
Rev. Harold Auler, Jr.	Ramseur, N.C.	United Church of Christ
Rev. John Austin	Paducah, Ky.	United Church of Christ

NAME	CITY	DENOMINATION
Franklin C. Basler	Tryon, N.C.	United Church of Christ
Warren Black	Webb, Miss.	United Methodist
Dr. Landrum Bolling	Washington, D.C.	Quaker
Rev. James Bracher	Carmel, Calif.	United Church of Christ
Rev. Theodore Braun	Carbondale, Ill.	United Church of Christ
Rev. John E. Buteyn	New York, N.Y.	Reformed Church in America
Ed Carlson	Rockford, Ill.	Salvation Army
Rev. Howard M. Caskey	Southampton, Pa.	United Methodist
Dale Christner	South Point, Ohio	Presbyterian, U.S.A.
Chuck Clark	Atlanta, Ga.	Nondenominational
Pat Clark	Woodstown, N.J.	American Baptist
Bishop Wayne Clymer	Minneapolis, Minn.	United Methodist
Dr. Lynn Coultas	Havana, Fla.	Presbyterian, U.S.
Rev. David Coulter	Brigham City, Utah	United Methodist
Marylou Crooks	Olivet, Mich.	United Church of Christ
John Dorean	Americus, Ga.	Presbyterian, U.S.A.
David Eastis	San José, Calif.	United Church of Christ
Venora Ellis	Westport, Conn.	Episcopal
Rev. Mark Frey	Robbins, Tenn.	United Church of Christ
Dr. David Geiger	New York, N.Y.	Presbyterian, U.S.A.
Rev. P.V. George	Plymouth, N.H.	United Church of Christ
Margaret Glocker	Vandalia, Ohio	Presbyterian, U.S.A.
Janice Gulezian	North Andover, Mass.	United Church of Christ
Rev. Keith Harris	Beaumont, Tex.	Southern Baptist
Kenneth Harris	Fallbrook, Calif.	American Baptist
Rev. David R. Holloway	Cumberland, Md.	Southern Baptist
Barbara Hoy	Fort Wayne, Ind.	United Church of Christ
Dr. Robert G. Johnson	Valley Forge, Pa.	American Baptist
Helen Kennedy	Lamar, Ind.	United Church of Christ
Joe Hershberger Kirk	Goshen, Ind.	Quaker
Junior Kreps	Vicksburg, Miss.	Christian Reformed Church
Rev. Bruce Larson	Seattle, Wash.	Presbyterian, U.S.A.
Albert Lee	Immokalee, Fla.	Pentecostal
Robert E. Leigh	Forest Hills, N.Y.	Congregational
Chris Lepp	Ontario, Canada	Mennonite
Dr. Ralph Loew	Buffalo, N.Y.	Lutheran Church in America
Pastor Lubuimi	Zaire, Africa	Baptist Community of Western Zaire
Birdie Lytle	San Antonio, Tex.	Presbyterian, U.S.A.
Rev. Ken MacHarg	Louisville, Ky.	United Church of Christ
Mary McCahon	Bayside, N.Y.	Congregational
Walter L. Maines	Rye, N.H.	United Church of Christ
Rev. Avery C. Manchester	New York, N.Y.	United Methodist
Robert D. Martin	Pigeon, Mich.	Mennonite
Joyce Millen	Harrisonburg, Va.	Mennonite
Cindy Miller	East Cleveland, Ohio	Presbyterian, U.S.A.
Rev. Roger Miller	Cincinnati, Ohio	United Church of Christ
Mary K. Monroe	Elmira, N.Y.	American Baptist

NAME	CITY	DENOMINATION
Nick Negrete	Denver, Colo.	Reformed Church in America
John Newell	Dayton, Ohio	American Baptist
Bob & Amy Olsen	Immokalee, Fla.	Church of the Brethren
Sandy Owen	Austin, Tex.	Disciples
Lucile Patrick	Delton, Mich.	Quaker
George Percival	Pleasant Hill, Tenn.	United Church of Christ
Jim Perigo	Evansville, Ind.	United Church of Christ
Rev. John Perkins	Jackson, Miss.	Baptist
Jim Ranck	John's Island, S.C.	Mennonite
Rev. Neill Richards	New York, N.Y.	United Church of Christ
Al Russell	Houston, Tex.	Disciples
Harry Sangree	Hanover, N.H.	United Church of Christ
Ken Sauder	Marietta, Pa.	Mennonite
Charles Schultz	Wichita, Kans.	American Baptist
Diane Scott	Salem, N.J.	American Baptist
Rev. Charles Selby	Luckey, Ohio	United Methodist
Dr. W. W. Sloan	Elon College, N.C.	United Church of Christ
Larry Stoner	Immokalee, Fla.	Mennonite
Kay Swicord	Brookeville, Md.	Presbyterian, U.S.A.
Dr. Clyde Tilley	Jackson, Tenn.	Southern Baptist
Dolores Van Loucks	Los Gatos, Calif.	United Church of Christ
Cynthia Wedel	Alexandria, Va.	Episcopal
Ralph Whittenburg	South Bend, Ind.	Lutheran Church in America
Bill Wiley	Zanesfield, Ohio	Presbyterian, U.S.A.
Earl Wilson	Indianapolis, Ind.	United Church of Christ
George Worth	Americus, Ga.	Presbyterian, U.S.
Dr. Donald Yates	Terre Haute, Ind.	Community Church
Dave Yutzy	Plain City, Ohio	Mennonite
Ben Zaglaniczny	Fort Myers, Fla.	Roman Catholic

Appendix D

Contributing Groups and Organizations

The groups and organizations that have contributed to the growing venture of Habitat for Humanity are too numerous to be listed in their entirety, but the following should be noted for their special and generous partnership with Habitat. Without them, this ministry would not be possible.

American Baptist Churches, U.S.A., Board of International Ministries
Christian Church (Disciples of Christ), Division of Overseas Ministries
Church of the Brethren
Eastern Mennonite Board of Missions and Charities
Friends World Committee for Consultation, Right Sharing of World Resources
Gemmer Christian Family Foundation
Hutterite colonies in North Dakota and in Manitoba, Canada
Lutheran Church in America, Division for World Mission and Ecumenism
Mennonite Central Committee
Reformed Church in America
United Church of Christ, United Church Board for World Ministries
United Evangelical Mission (West Germany)
United Methodist Church, United Methodist Committee on Relief
United Presbyterian Church, Self Development of People Fund
Zaire Protestant Relief Agency (Kinshasa, Zaire)

Appendix E

Designated Gifts

Special gifts, designated for a particular purpose, or in memory of a loved one, or to honor someone, comprise a significant portion of Habitat's support. There have been too many of these to list them all, but a few examples are noteworthy:

A grant of $2,000 voted by the Indiana-Kentucky Conference of the United Church of Christ at its 1979 meeting, presented at the dedication service in Ntondo, Zaire (July 1979), to build a house in honor of Dr. Harry Bredeweg, conference minister, and his wife Imogene.

Designated gifts of $1,000 and $5,000 from Dr. and Mrs. W. W. Sloan of Elon College, North Carolina, providing **1.** seed money for a Habitat project in Zambia (not yet started as this book goes to press), and **2.** the first two houses in the Kinshasa, Zaire, project.

A gift of 5,000 trees from the International Women's Club of Kinshasa, Zaire, for beautification and erosion control at the Habitat project site.

A designated grant of $7,000, raised by Habitat board president Sam Emerick, for a new clinic in the Kinshasa project.

Special gifts, totaling $2,200, for a pickup truck for the Habitat building crew in Americus, Georgia, contributed by churches in Charlotte, North Carolina; Goshen, LaPorte, Indianapolis, Muncie, Anderson, and Hagerstown, Indiana; Belmont, Massachusetts; Clemson, South Carolina; and West Bloomfield, Michigan.

Designated gifts of $1,500 each from Olivet Presbyterian Church, Evansville, Indiana; First Congregational Church, Dupo, Illinois; Grace Mennonite Church, Pandora, Ohio; Bethany Congregational United Church of Christ, Rye, New Hampshire ($3,000, for two houses); Memorial Boulevard Christian Church, St. Louis, Missouri; Mr. & Mrs. Herbert Myers, Jr., Mount Joy, Pennsylvania; Mr. & Mrs. Andrew H. Gibson, Midland, Michigan; Don MacFarlane, Janesville, Wisconsin; and Mr. & Mrs. Richard Palmiter, Toledo, Ohio, for the first ten houses in the Aguacatan, Guatemala, Habitat project.